Under American Skies

Under American Skies

Francesca Andreini

Translation by Samantha Traxler

Washington, DC

Copyright © 2021 by Francesca Andreini

New Academia Publishing, 2021

Originally published in Italian by Edizioni del Gattaccio in 2015, with the title, *Primi anni a WDC*

Translation into English by Samantha Traxler

All rights reserved. No part of this book may be reproduced or transmitted in any form or by any means, electronic or mechanical, including photocopying, recording, or by any information storage and retrieval system, without permission in writing from the copyright owner

Printed in the United States of America

Library of Congress Control Number: 2021942379
ISBN 978-1-7359378-9-2 (alk. paper)

 SCARITH is an imprint of New Academia Publishing

New Academia Publishing
4401-A Connecticut Ave. NW #236, Washington DC 20008
info@newacademia.com - www.newacademia.com

To my parents,
Fiorenza and Mario

Contents

Preface ix

Chapter I 1
Chapter II 33
Chapter III 61
Chapter IV 83
Chapter V 121
Chapter VI 153

Notes 185

"Kathy I'm lost," I said, though I knew she was sleeping
"I'm empty and aching and I don't know why"
Counting the cars on the New Jersey Turnpike
They've all come to look for America
All come to look for America
All come to look for America

Simon and Garfunkel, *America*

Preface

by Raimondo Bultrini

Andreini's book is rich and dense, but also gifted with the light, lavish euphoria of discovery. Her America is a kaleidoscope of different moods and features—from the more superficial to the deepest strata of society—describing all the beliefs, conditionings, contradictions, vices and virtues of a great country which is perpetually transforming.

Her tone is light and often ironic in dealing with the theme of human suffering through her authentic, first-hand experience as an expatriate. She goes beyond just being content with her discoveries and doesn't judge her new surroundings with indifference, rather by intimately participating in them.

Her careful, sensitive, but sometimes stern gaze is poised on people and events, always questioning whilst acknowledging she will never know enough to fully embrace the wonder and joys of each new disclosure. Her writing flows, relaxed and lyrical, considering the vastness and variety of natural attractions as well as the rich and complex humanity they contain. Her measure is the awareness of dealing with a different space, which requires a new outlook on reality, setting everything in its place, and where opportunities have always been sketched by the possibility of finding a "new space" to express themselves.

What is available to Americans which is unknown to those of us from the Old Continent? And what, instead, have the Americans forsaken? What could they recover from the culture they left behind?

The understanding, questioning and analysis of the New World is, however, not the focus of her book: rather the twisting and turning through the essential traits of the author's personal, domestic and most intimate dimensions. The everyday experiences, a challenging illness, the kids' schooling, and the difficulty in relating to others, echo more dramatically when in a foreign land, far away from one's usual support system, surrounded by unknown social codes and idioms which are alien to our lives—normally based on acquired certainties.

New awareness and new solutions are born thanks to this totally estranging experience and the loss of the support of those comforting mental mechanisms which she could count on before. So the author—and with her the reader—can now discover unexplored dimensions of consciousness.

CHAPTER I

Off we go

The other travelers look at their watches, check the departure boards and take off in a hurry, grasping the handles of their suitcases. Some, in transit, remain seated, crunching morsels of snacks and tiredness, among tangles of luggage, arms hanging low, magazines and whining kids. The heat, in Fiumicino, followed everyone deep into the airport, hidden under summer clothes, and is now seeping out of every movement.

It hangs over the five of us too, as we take up a whole row of seats. We, the grown-ups, are strewn with bags and shoulder straps; the children, dressed in multiple layers of clothes, are ready to endure all temperatures. Slightly pale, slightly crumpled by a spring full of commitments, we now sit transfixed, holding essential things such as laptops, contracts, bookings and teddy bears. The usual mini move that takes off with us with every relocation.

My youngest daughter looks at me, flushed.
"Mum, can I take my vest off at least?"
"Where are we going to put it? Have a bit of patience, we'll be going soon. Maybe if I move this you'll be more comfortable… ok?" I answer while repositioning the large suitcase between us.
"How old are they?" the petite woman sitting opposite asks.
I smile: "Five, ten and thirteen."
"Traveling must be a business."
I shrug, we're used to it.
The woman seems perplexed by the number of offspring and objects we have in tow. I wonder what she would have thought seeing us a few years ago when we travelled with two strollers and our youngest on a leash. Or even just a few minutes ago, when our cat was still with us, glaring straight out of her crate, a deep desperate sound gushing from her throat.

To put the crate through the scanner, we had to extract her then shove her back in amid panicky screams, scratches, attempted breakaways and cursing.

Now, she's lingering in some depot in the special luggage unit. And we are sitting here. Still.

"Why do we have to leave?" the little one asks. Again.

"Because it's fun," I repeat. "Because Dad was offered a great job, and we'll do lots of new stuff…"

Because the money has dried up, my love. Because for the past five years I've been soaking up Rome with its lights and commotion, as if it were a feeding bottle full of noise and chaos, meetings and vibrant days. Because I've spent nights writing and breathing sleep as if it were rare oxygen. Because a plethora of obligations have sent Mum and Dad down two separate, steep paths we couldn't take our eyes off.

And the time has come for us to invent ourselves a new life, together.

The airport moves around us while others are stirring. The children stretch the fatigue out of their muscles.

"And now, what do we do?" the eldest daughter asks.

"We wait, that's all we can do."

We, the parents, interlace our scratched fingers and look straight ahead, like bewildered cats.

We have spent weeks saying goodbye to friends, teachers and relatives, cancelling utilities, subscriptions and engagements. Changing services, closing accounts. We were cautious and started ahead of time; this isn't our first relocation after all. Let's take our time, we told ourselves, and do everything right. Even so. These last weeks, matters which hadn't been dealt with suddenly cropped up, so we had to put things right, run around hurriedly and make more phone calls.

Like a dervish getting caught in a crescendo of whirling spires, or a first time wizard who doesn't know how to stop a spell, we threw our lives into a spinning vortex that frantically tore away our habits, our certainties and everything we had built over the last few years. Like magicians and exalted dancers, we dizzied ourselves for weeks with tasks, throwing ourselves into this rush towards a new path.

Right up to this morning, this airport, these smelly seats that feel like the eye of the cyclone, where everything is suddenly still and flat.

Now we can rest, hold hands and wait.

Watch the hurricane we ourselves have put into motion, still whirling around us, hurling everything away.

A friendly face, a regular hangout, the smell of a hug, the fountain at the end of the road, the pigeons wetting their heads, the gravel underfoot, the leaves which have lived through changing seasons, the flowerbeds in the park, the children's games, the curls of the little boy who says goodbye without smiling, "Are you really leaving?"

Everything is spinning and moving into the distance; our former life rapidly disappearing into a blurry mist.

We let ourselves be distracted by some magazines, the hustle and bustle around us, the comics and games crumpled up halfheartedly. We, the adults, check the tickets and documents one last time, answer a few last messages from friends and colleagues.

I'm startled by a number appearing on my phone, take a breath and answer.

It's great to hear your voice, of course I'm happy to be going… Of course I'm sorry.

"You'll see, it'll be great, I'm sure you'll find something interesting to do. It's just too bad you're leaving, we were a great team, you and I…"

As I end the call, I see two years of work falling apart, breaking away and flying off my fingertips into the hurricane, with everything else. I won't be contributing to the final draft; someone else will be wrapping up the film project. I've been running like a child at the top of my lungs and, now that the kite is finally in the air, I have to open my hands and let it fly away…

"The passengers going to Washington are kindly asked to head to boarding."

Finally.

"Kids, let's get going."

We all pick up our too many bags.

"Have we got everything? Are you sure?"

Bearing excessive weight, we all walk along like drunken ducks towards the gate, pass the airline desk and make our way along the bridge.

The little one pulls my sleeve.

"Mum?"

I dislodge my backpack to get a better look at him.

"Yes, my love?"

"Will my fish be happy in your friend's pond?"

I smile at him.

"Of course… He'll have the time of his life!"

I turn to the girls who were listening carefully without saying a word, and smile at them too.

As we advance through the cabin crew's welcoming ritual, I catch my husband's eye. Every few years he carts us all off to live somewhere far away. Now, he's glancing at me, wondering whether—once again—I'm actually in the mood for smiling.

Then, in the plane, having ditched our heavy bags and fastened our seat belts, we all doze off. Biting the bullet of our adieus in solitude. Each one of us, flattened against his seat, tasting the chagrin of taking off.

I don't look out as Rome grows smaller and farther away below us. Instead, with my eyes closed, I think of the objects, the faces, the rooms and the sensations which have suddenly become my past.

As we climb higher and higher, they hover over me, like a friendly ghost who doesn't want to fly away into nothingness.

The wooden floor steeped in the meals we cooked, games we played, pets' paw marks and baby vomit… The unique blend is still there, where we left it a few hours ago. But it's already far away. In the past.

I wonder how the cat is doing. She must be meowling desperately, locked up in her crate. Anyway, no one can hear her, stored away in the hold, like any other piece of luggage. And, she has no distant present to deal with. She carries her present around with her, at all times, doesn't have to worry about putting it into perspective or making connections, explaining or expecting anything. She's in the hold, suffering, crushed by the noise and lack of oxygen, with her common-luggage present upon herself.

We soon reach cruising altitude and the food carts, with boiling hot smells, start coming through. The ritual of routine questions and extended arms begins.

We drink wine or coca cola, and open the boiling hot containers.

"It doesn't look too bad, right kids?"

Then we slip on our earphones and tune into the tiny screens in front of us. It feels as if our lives depend upon watching everything we can watch and eating everything we can eat.

Each one of us now clutching the distant fragrances, lights and faces we have left behind.

"We'll do lots of fun stuff in the US!" we, the parents, tell the kids, between a film and a meal.

We describe what the distant present suggests our future will be like: a life that is just as remote and imperceptible, and so unknown it seems impossible, but which will come true, some day.

"We won't have the same old habits, but we'll take trips and go on adventures. It won't be Rome, but it'll be big cities and really tall skyscrapers. And new people, not just the usual faces."

People of all kinds and strange people no one turns around to look at, because that's what happens in the States. You can dress the way you want. Do what you want. Speak your mind. No one's blown away and, if they are, they keep it to themselves. They just say hi and smile because that's the way it is, everyone says hi and smiles.

"Why do they always smile?"

"Because people in the States are welcoming. They're open."

They are kind and easygoing. And practical: everything works well and is easy to use. The United States is fun, and comfortable. We've told you over and over again; we grownups have been there and really liked it. We travelled around quite a bit, and saw beautiful places.

"I don't want to see beautiful places!"

"Of course you do! We'll take a lot of trips!"

We'll see great open spaces, so vast you feel lost in them. Highways so long you never meet another car and feel free. Motels with signs on the road telling you if they have vacancies and how much they cost; you don't even need to get out of the car! And these motels are everywhere, you don't need to plan ahead. Everything is so easy in the States. You'll see.

Grated parmesan

"Look, there it is!"

"Where are the skyscrapers?"

"Mum, Dad, where are the skyscrapers? Why can't I see any skyscrapers, Mum?"

Skyscrapers are everywhere in the States and in many other countries in Asia, the Middle East, even in Africa by now. But not in Washington.

Washington, from the airplane, looks just like the satellite view on the computer screen: a lush, dark green, tropical stretch of land.

"It must rain a lot around here..." I think, faced with all that green.

Then it dawns on me: that green place, where it rains a lot, is about to become "our" home. So I ask the first steward walking by for another glass of wine.

As the airplane descends, the green turns into trees, grass and hedges, and in between the trees, grass and hedges, some light colored houses start standing out. Not too close to one another and lined up, along roads that seem to have no beginning and no end.

Getting closer, we can spot the white picket fences, the garages and the driveways, cropping up throughout the green of the trees, plants and grass. As if some mischievous rascal had taken one of our cities, from over there in old, overcrowded Europe, crumbled it up in the palm of his hand and scattered it around, here and there, on a vast green expanse.

Empty nature with a sprinkling of houses.

That's my impression as we are about to land in the place we'll be living in for the next few years. And I walk down the jetway picturing a plate of pasta sprinkled with grated parmesan.

Then we walk out of the airport with the cat in her crate hurling insults and desperation. We are probably just as loud as she is, calling out orders and instructions, grabbing things. Catch up, watch out for the cars, look where you're going and say sorry! Didn't you see the man?
"Sorry, I'm so sorry... Kids, be careful!"
The crate weighs a ton, but it was the only way we could bring the cat with us. The American airline gave us no choice: we were only allowed the old, outdated, heavy, expensive kind, with bolts and screws. And I wonder how anyone elderly could actually manage to drag their cat along with them—in such a heavy crate—down this long narrow corridor that winds around the airport. It seems to never end, and has no other exits, no moving walkways, just walls and doors which sometimes open, letting loose passengers from another flight—and you have to watch you don't get separated in the crowd or get lost, or end up stepping on a child's foot or with your stomach under some teenager's backpack.
"But isn't the United States supposed to be so efficient?" my mischievous brain chimes in. And I tell it to shut up, we're going to be just fine here and there's nothing wrong with a few irrational things in the beginning. We are going to be just fine.

As with the crate, there's another piece of luggage we hadn't taken into account: tropical heat. When we come out onto the street, it grabs us by the shoulders and doesn't let go, hugs and embraces us, as if we had adopted a bothersome little monkey. While the bags and the suitcases weigh down our tired arms, already worn out by the long hours of travel, the little monkey grips us and takes our strength away. Sometimes it climbs down our necks and jumps all over our suitcases, making them so heavy we can hardly drag them along.
We walk and walk, sweat pouring down our strained necks.
"'No Country For Old Men'—no wonder, only young guys can survive this kind of haul!" we the parents comment, jokingly.

Meanwhile, we walk along overpasses, and underpasses, catch a bus, get off the bus until "Finally!" we find the car rental office. One bureaucratic setback later ("What? Can this be worse than in Italy?!"), we get our car and drive into the city.

"Where are the skyscrapers?"

It's me wondering this time. The kids, in their infinite wisdom, have understood that grownups have a vast repertoire of "things they just say" and have filed away almost everything we've told them over the past few months. They start chatting among themselves and playing video games.

We grownups watch the dense green wall of very tall trees that are still lining the road we have been traveling along since the airport. Miles and miles and not even a crack in the green wall. Nothing to see, no sign of a civilization unlike our own. Or even similar. Beautiful or ugly, or peculiar, or just different. Green is green and the leaves are leaves and we could have landed in the Amazon for all we know. Maybe we have.

"Look, the skyscrapers!"

The enthusiasm is suddenly back. After passing some isolated warehouses and an empty baseball field, the green brush is gone and we are, all of a sudden, on streets which intersect other streets.

We've reached Silver Spring, a town near Washington where we'll be spending our first few weeks. In the only apartment we'd managed to find, for a reasonable price, and which allowed a cat.

My wicked brain whispers that maybe I should have started having doubts about everything being so easy and welcoming in the States before even getting to the airport. While I had spent long nights searching and it seemed I couldn't find a roof to put over our heads for love or money. Even the families of my husband's colleagues, who had been through the same problem, were unable to help.

"You need time and luck. It took us three months," they told us.

I only had a handful of days and sleepless nights.

Silver Spring has a fair supply of skyscrapers; six or seven, all standing together, so it looks like more. And it really is full of differently colored people.

On our first evening exploring, we walk around, satisfied, among all the multiethnic faces and clothes.

We point out the Indian women in their colorful saris and the tiny asian women, to the kids. The blond, red and brown haired people. Some latinos with the facial features of ancient forsaken American civilizations. And lots of black people; I'd only ever seen so many when we lived in Dakar. Here in Silver Spring, they seem to be the majority. It brings back the feeling I'd had in Africa of living in an upside down world: everything which was once one color, is now the opposite. And it feels surprisingly like home.

We come across a group of African Americans who have gathered a little crowd around them. They are holding signs with drawings of Neanderthal men and slogans saying that we, white people, are like those guys: dumb and evil. Other posters show pictures of Hitler and World War 2, and the African Americans holding them are shouting that this is the world, this is white people's history.

Our kids look at the crowd with the posters and smile at them because they don't understand what the protesters are saying.

We tell them to stop smiling, because they might think we are making fun of them.

"Making fun of them, why?"

"It's a bit hard to explain…"

As we walk by, I think of all the wars white men have waged and are still waging. Yes, they are right. Right to insult us for all those horrible things we have done. I walk ahead, feeling good, because I agree.

It's a midsummer evening. There is still a lot of light and lots of people are out on the streets.

Everyone has his own little monkey around his neck, and is doing what he can to shake it off. A little boy on a skateboard glides, slowly, through the crowd. An Arab mother sits with a baby in her arms, fanning herself with the hem of her hijab. A group of bare-chested teenagers stroll by, holding enormous cups of icy soda.

Others lean against the walls or sit on the steps of this little square decorated with red bricks, signs, and several bright lit cafés.

People greet one another in the evening heat, in slow, low voices.

"Hey!" "Hi!" "Hiya doin'?"

The monosyllabic words struggle to find their way from one person to the other.

In the middle of the square, a fountain gushes water high into the sky, before letting it fall in a loud shower all around. It's a fountain with no edges and no fixed perimeter, with water pouring down, spreading out on the tiny multicolored tiles outlining its base, flowing away and evaporating. A dozen kids in their underwear are running around under the spray laughing, splashing and having fun.

My little one looks at me and I smile with my consent. Then again, he's too new here. And his body is telling him it's two o'clock in the morning, not eight pm as they say it is here. So we sit down on the steps nearby and watch the kids playing. At some point, a chubby boy with flabs of fat around his waist, hips, chest, and right up to his neck, sits on the fountain, right on top of the water spout. The spray stops and silence falls. Then a few kids, who were splashing around, start complaining that there's no water.

My kids are now laughing noisily and we scold them. Others could think we are laughing at his physique and that wouldn't be kind.

The other kids in their underwear take off to splash around in the other smaller fountains nearby, leaving the fat boy to plug the main spout for as long as he wants. So he sits there, proud of the momentous impact of his backside. Then he stands up and joins the others.

I don't know why, but I feel sure this will always be one of our first memories of the United States, even in the years to come.

The second one will be the first day of school

Long strips of yellow plastic tape suddenly appear beyond the windshield, as I come out of the garage. I've just driven on to the street and find myself wrapped in all this cheerful tape fluttering in the wind. It's everywhere: stretched between lampposts and street signs, as well as from one building to another. Like decorations.

A small crowd of pedestrians files along the sidewalk, brushing the tape with their chests while scanning the area with watchful eyes.

Is this an art installation?

It's the first thing that comes to mind, as I awkwardly try to come to terms with all the tape and the people standing by. Then I notice the policemen clad in riot shields and helmets, and the helicopters hovering low, around the skyscrapers. They fly over and over the roofs of each building, including the one I'm driving out of.

Yes, we are living in a skyscraper now. When we arrived, we discovered that the little apartment we had rented from Rome was in one of those brick buildings with thousands of windows.

Entering the rooms full of light and sky, we dropped our luggage and gave in to our surprise.

"It's so cool, Mum! Did you know?"

"No, I had no idea… It's beautiful."

We are on a lower floor but the other skyscrapers are all around us and the impact is guaranteed. The large windows, giving onto the roads below, make us feel as if we were in a reversed aquarium: we, the spectators, are inside and the show is out there, in the urban landscape. The streets, ninety-degree crossroads, cars and pedestrians who take turns at the traffic lights, the windows of the other buildings through which we can hint at what is happening inside… People's lives are so easy to observe: so vulnerable.

In the buildings opposite, we watch the morning ritual of windows being shielded from the ruthless sun followed by the loud whirring of the air conditioners (hung by the hundreds, one at every window). In the evening, the ritual of curtains being pulled open, as pools of light flood down from the neon ceiling lights onto half-empty rooms.

Rituals which our residential skyscraper shares with the offices in the buildings opposite.

And with the Discovery Channel skyscraper nearby, where TV documentaries are made.

Their skyscraper has a bogus shark stuck to it, stretched across the facade: the torso and tail hanging out one side, the head and wide open jaws sticking out the other side. We would often stop to examine it from below. Our noses in the air, looking at the long white teeth and the deep red throat, gaping wide, some twenty meters above the pedestrians.

Right now people have their noses in the air, but this time they are looking at the helicopters instead of the shark. They fly back and forth, and their very loud flap flap sound is covered, now and again, by the wailing of the police sirens, the ambulances and the armed forces.

No, it can't be an art installation after all... So, what's happening?

"Somebody has kidnapped a few Discovery Channel employees. The whole building has been evacuated, apart from the Discovery offices," my husband explains from his office.

I'd called to tell him I was stuck behind the tape. So he'd turned the television on and seen the images from the helicopters: our skyscraper and the neighboring ones being surrounded by a large contingent of law enforcement.

Because no one knows who's in that building, if there are others nearby or if they want to blow something up...

Meanwhile, the school bus with our kids is on its way back, full of all the worried thoughts, tensions and events they have lived through, on their own, during their very long first day without their friends, their usual points of reference and stomping grounds. With only one certainty they could rely on: Mum, at the bus stop, to greet them with her arms open, ready for their inevitable sulking.

But their Mum still has to get through the tape. She's been told that American policemen are nervous, so she mustn't make any sudden or reckless movements; always speak calmly and keep her hands in sight because you never know what could happen.

Still, however hard she tries, the only sound coming out of her locked jaw is a desperately mumbled explanation of her plight. And, instead of looking like an upright citizen, she has the frantic glare of a crazy woman ready to blow herself up if she can't get to her children in time.

Otherwise they'll be left on the sidewalk without knowing what has happened or how to ask for an explanation. Without knowing where they are and whether anyone will ever pick them up.

"Officer, I beg you…"

Their Mum watches the glitzy mirrored sunglasses, the stiff posture of the uniform, and understands the policeman won't listen to pity, he'll only follow orders.

He observes her from behind his expressionless glasses. Evaluates. Talks into a headset.

Then, finally, one hand lifts the tape in front of the windshield while the other hand signals her to go, quickly.

Soon after, another uniform lifts another tape while another hand signals to hurry up. Then one more, and again another.

And she is out from behind the tape.

As she struggles through the swell of cars that are jammed together from various directions under the glistening heat, scenes from the last few nights come to mind. The sleepless children, with swollen eyes, making long lists of all the people they have left in Rome and won't be joining on their first day of school. Everything they won't see. Everything they won't do.

She mustn't be late.

So she reclaims all the subtleties and forbidden tricks, learnt in the many years of driving in African and Middle Eastern countries, where getting through traffic jams is a perpetual and regular norm, not a mere setback. And in Rome, where gridlock is a daily affair even if people consider it an unacceptable holdup to be forcefully expelled from their lives.

Taking stock of the years spent with tires up on traffic islands, squiggly detours and forbidden turns, their Mum arrives at the bus stop only one hour late. But calm enough because her brain, in the meantime, has told her that the school bus must have also been caught up in the traffic jam.

And her brain is right this time: when the noisy, smelly yellow bus arrives, she is already there, her arms are open, and she is ready to take on and diffuse all the sulking.

The third memory: Maine

The cool and stretched out state of Maine we drove through for long hours of endless daylight. The sun shimmering on the woods, ocean and rocky coves.

Later, back in the skyscraper, we often talk about Maine and the heart-wrenching nostalgia it left us with: the clear air, beautiful calm boats anchored to the piers, large wooden mansions, freshly painted and spotless, surrounded by stunningly kept flower gardens.

Houses we'd often stopped to admire, photograph and compare, during our first hours on the road.

"I like that yellow one best!"

"I like the one with the windows on the roof!"

"I like the one with the porch!"

The one with the wild flowers in the flowerbed, the one with the tree house and the one with the American flag hanging from the balcony…

The balconies, porches, tree houses and American flags appearing over and over again.

The mansions in Maine are differentiated by an infinite score of small variations. Just like in any residential American suburb, but with a neater shine and sharper colours. I suppose it comes from the surrounding landscape, so briny, clean and fresh, it reflects on the way everything has been conceived: the houses, the boats, the piers and even the restaurants inside wooden verandas, stretching out to sea.

Nonetheless, somewhere along the trip, we got bored with all the variations and the straight lines, symmetry and spotlessness. We stopped making comparisons, taking pictures or even commenting. The children drew on their paper pads. We and the friends from Italy who had joined us for the trip, looked at the maps.

Meanwhile, other tourists continued jumping in and out of their cars, calling out "Oh, look at that one!" while looking at the various porches, gardens, flags and sky windows. Dreaming of the privileged existence of the owners of this or that fairy-tale mansion set among a cluster of rocks, looking out over the ocean. The white lighthouse nearby and the seagulls swooping overhead, crying out to the waves. Mansions which also have small sandy coves, tucked into the rocks nearby, where the residents can stretch out to sunbathe.

"And you never get sunburnt here! You can play ball without sweating and picnic on the sand without sunscreen on your hands!" as my American friend from Italy commented, perfectly at ease with the scenery around us.

Neither she nor the other visitors seemed at all bothered by this sort of private property which, instead, made me more and more outraged. Because there are notions such as coastline, shore, rocks and woods which, in my view, can't be paired with the idea that someone has taken possession of *that* coastline, *that* shore, *those* rocky boulders and least of all *those* woods. Which is exactly what the owners of these wonderful variations of American homes do, without worrying about environmental or moral issues.

I can't be passionate about a wonder I can't enjoy. What's the point in looking at a shore when you can't dip your feet in its water? Or a meal without sunscreen and sunburns in a cove if you're not even allowed to walk through it, even when it's not fenced off.

We had already been forced away from another heavenly niche—a clearing in the woods with a lake and water lilies.

"This isn't a park! It's private property!" the owner had barked at us.

So we'd collected our shoes and bags, sandwiches and laughs, caught the kids, who were running after one another through the trees, and thrown everything back into the car.

Why was that guy so upset? How were we supposed to know that Bambi's forest belonged to someone?

"Why don't they use fences?! That way we'd know," I blurted out, disappointed that our bucolic idyll had been interrupted.

"It's not what people do here. They don't close areas off!" my friend told me.

"Private property is off limits, here. Everyone knows it, so there's no need to protect it," her husband added.

So, I stepped onto the accelerator and drove the wheels and

my nerves to the first spot that was neither fenced nor belonged to anybody because it belonged to everyone.

And on that gigantic stretch of fresh sand we ran, with the briny wind blowing on our faces and our mouths full of screams and laughter. We swam in the cold water, sunbathed without getting sunburnt and smelt the rosehip that stretched, as far as the eye could see, over the large bushes skirting the sand dunes.

Days with a tail wrapped around them

Back in the skyscraper, we cuddle up together in the place the kids now call our *homey home*. They really like it because it's small, lined with soft carpeting, has new furniture and large windows. But the cat is bored out of her wits. She can't go out; for the first time in her short cat life she can't even put a paw out into the open air.

Almost all skyscraper windows are sealed and those that do open a small crack, give on to a void. The cat looks at us, dejected, then solemnly wraps her tail around her down time, places it meticulously on her front paws and squints at the surroundings with her eyes half shut.

My husband was the first to start wandering about, getting to know places. He would go out early and come back late, and threw himself into his job as if it were a passing spaceship. One haul, no layovers: home–work–home. He thrust himself into a galaxy we know nothing about, where he meets people, does things, produces, he's useful and active, looks around and understands. He already knows how to find his way around and refers to places, explains routes and situations.

I, instead, look around the reversed aquarium, observe the kids playing and sit next to the cat. I wish I had a tail I could wrap around my hands.

I look at the building where the madman took the employees hostage on the first day of school.

They weren't terrorists and weren't even numerous. Just a lone, loony preservationist who attacked the documentary producing channel to make people aware of environmental issues. But, because he did it while pointing a gun at the staff, no one even listened or understood. They shot him, killed him, and it was all over. A sigh of relief, the tape comes down, the helicopters land and people with their noses in the air go home.

They've also taken the decoration down: no more shark stretched over the building now, just a cementified normality.

All around, buildings and skyscrapers stand, alternating solid blocks and more blocks, creating an immense, right-angled prospect. In between these blocks, along short inclines which are either grey or green, streets and parks open onto large roads with vehicles, shops and walkways.

I'm surprised by the fact people here spend their everyday lives in these boundless planes, going in and out of these gigantic cubes. Maybe all this magnitude explains why everyone hurries around in a rush with a seemingly precise goal in mind, knowing exactly how to reach it.

Everyone.

Every mother, with her child in her arms or in a stroller, slung to her chest or her back, looking either overcome, kind, anxious or in a rush.

Every teenager, clutching the books which hold his future, or busying himself with some part time job to scrape together a bit of small cash.

Every elderly person, his old age dragged around on a senior's scooter or by a dog's leash.

Every father, dutifully showing he actually enjoys doing his bit while holding his kids' hands on swimming-lessons afternoons or, at the other end of a pitch, catching a ball, on playtime afternoons.

Kids aren't "every kid," they're always "the kids."

In the fenced school yards, in the parks running around playing games, pushing one another on swings, or faced with an adult's reproach in the street, the children are a collective entity, they're the kids. Probably putting together "his" or "her" future. But not each one for himself; they do things within a loud chorus of voices, faces and different languages. All together in their common childhood experience, collectively.

But what is it that holds together the others, the American adults, in this part of the States?

The air seems rarefied around here, made up of individual goals. And, here and there, a few soft gusts of principles that are so openly exhibited they don't seem quite genuine.

Especially now, with the election campaign in full swing and proclamations posted on every street corner.

In November, the House of Representatives and part of the Senate, some governors and some state legislatures will be up for re-election.

The usual midterm turnover is predicted, with the opposition party overthrowing the incumbent. But judging by the passion both Republican and Democrat candidates put into competing for each pedestrian's vote, all bets are off.

Smiling impersonators, dressed like the political nominee they are campaigning for, hold up placards with the party's slogans, and wave at everyone. Spotless billboards spell out the names of one or more candidates (It's so unlike Italy, where campaign posters are torn, covered in graffiti or glued on top of one another to hide the other candidate's face or message). Then, these same names—always the same—are printed on bumper stickers and leaflets left in the mailbox, or called out in recorded telephone messages that start playing as soon as you lift the receiver.

And that's not the only campaign taking place.

Every day, a man parades along one of the main avenues with a placard against pedophilia among the clergy. He was molested as a child and for years now he has been protesting in front of the Apostolic Nunciature.

Not to mention the banners in favor of Israel outside synagogues. Or the words of Christ posted outside churches for the christians.

Everyone has the right to speak up, everyone has his own message.

Everyone.

"People here really can say what they want!" my children comment. In Italy, they'd learnt to hide their opinions to be well received. Now, in this part of the world, they're surprised by what people get away with declaring.

"In Italy, they would have scribbled all over that poster," they observe.

"And that guy would have been beaten up sooner or later," they infer.

Here instead, on trimmed front lawns, small shiny metal signs shoot up unscathed with the names of congressional candidates. Rivals of different colors, with opposing slogans, stand side by side, in neighboring gardens, competing for the attention of anyone passing by. Everyone with his own private property and his individual political opinion.

We see lots of these signs, more and more of them, as we move away from Silver Spring, and its downtown skyscrapers, looking for a house in Washington's residential neighborhoods and suburbs.

The kids complain: "Why can't we stay in our homey home?" But the location isn't right, it's too far from school and the apartment is just too small. We must explore.

Driving around in our rental car, we travel into neighborhoods we can't even pinpoint on a map, back and forth through woods that appear out of the blue ("How many parks are there in this city?!?"), along highways and into vast expanses strewn with little houses that all look almost identical.

We discover that in and around Washington there are only a few properties available, with all the agencies fiercely competing for them. And, they are off the market in a matter of hours. Choosing a house in these circumstances is like playing Russian roulette. When you still can't find your way around ("Is the school near or far from here?"), you have no idea what services are at hand ("Where do people shop around here?") and while you are standing there thinking about it, the dispirited realtor looks at you, his mobile phone in hand.

"I'm sorry, I've just been told this house is no longer available. We should hurry to the next one."

Finally, Lady Luck smiles down on us. On a day of torrential rain, we too find the American home that suits us.

Wooden and with a garden, a gray roof, painted siding and a pretty balcony.

A white house, looking old and wise, greets us. Sheltered by the surrounding tall trees, it promises silent evenings and cosy fireplaces.

But it has neither the candid Maine sheen nor the gracious neatness of the other houses on the street. What with too many former leases and its owner having turned a blind eye for years, it looks slightly neglected and ailing.

We have very few alternatives but some negotiation is still called for.

"It needs a lot of work, we can't take it in these conditions."
"The owner has no intention of refurbishing, I'm sorry."
"What a pity."
"Otherwise, could you deal with the renovation yourselves?"

So, we decide to take the work on ourselves. To stop the charm of better times becoming a swarm of termites, and keep the drains and the creaking within the normal range of a house with "some character."

With the help of a team of tireless Peruvians, we sand away the rust from the elaborate ironwork, waterproof the beams, and replace the windows covered in webs of cracks. We scrub away, wax, paint, air every corner of the house in a tidying frenzy that brings to mind an old fashioned village spring-cleaning. But, instead of holy water and prayers[1], we are blessed, in the end, with a twenty foot container unloading itself into the empty rooms.

Suddenly the cyclone is hailing everything back at us: objects, clothes, medicines, tights, combs, games, books, notebooks and heaven knows how many things we have been dragging around the world for years. A bit more ruined at each time, a bit more opaque and fed up with being shipped around and dealing with different climates. Having moaned in the damp, cracked in the drought, lost color in the scorching heat or been tarnished by the cold, depending on where the hurricane had flung them in the past.

"Here's the kitchenware!"
"I've found the books!"

We knife open the boxes with a kind of Dionysian glee. With more and more expertise and speed, we dive our hands into the soft polystyrene packaging and pull out letter openers, nasal sprays, wool sweaters and poolside flip flops. The usual stuff that gets thrown into boxes in a hurry, when even hesitating between "Should I keep it or throw it out?" costs time and money, and in the end it all ends up in the cauldron.

Then we kneel down to gut the larger loads and free our home's sacred objects from multiple layers of cardboard and paper.

Bookshelves. Sofas. Dining room table. Beds.

We bow down to nourish and polish them with bee's wax, offer incense and scented candles to give thanks: everything is here and nothing's been broken.

One afternoon, boxes and box cutters still in our hands, the next door neighbors pay us a visit. Very kind and discreet, they provide us with cookies and photos of their family, each one's name written underneath. Covered in sweat, we relax our faces and beam because this is a prophecy come true: the kind Americans really are welcoming us warm-heartedly.

"Thank you, see you soon!" we call out as they walk away.

Our words expressing a vision: let's take a break, every now and then, to have a chat with them; get to know them and let them get to know us, build a friendship. Get their advice and pick up some tips. Watch our little one play with their three boys who are more or less his age.

But, within a few days, our dreams crash into a fence of reality.

The neighbors go about their business, discreet, proactive, according to their schedules and habits. Their routines are unchanged by this external event: the sudden arrival of a clan of strangers next door. They decline our invitations and, a few times, send back my little boy who had gone over to suggest an afternoon of fun and games, because it just wasn't a good time for them.

On the other hand, during one of our first unplanned encounters in the street, I realize we too disappoint them.

The mother tells me she keeps her two youngest at home and teaches them herself.

"Really?"

"Yes, it's a common practice here in the States. It's called homeschooling. But our eldest goes to the local school, so I'm sure we'll meet there. What after school activities do your kids do?"

"Our kids go to an international school…" I answer.

With just one sentence, a common ground made of school programs, recitals, meetings and pick-ups is swept away.

"Yes, well, I understand…" she adds and bends over to pick up her last-born child.

Then she brightens up: "Well, anyway, we'll see you in church on Sunday. Do you go to the one down the road?"

"Actually… no, we don't.»

At this point, all she has left is a polite glint of a smile. I understand she'll always grant me a kind thought and a considerate word, but access to friendship will invariably be denied.

We continue unpacking, cleaning and tidying up. Tired and glum, we have dinner on the floor, surrounded by boxes and wrapping. And a sole distraction: our stupefied cat wandering around, hiding in every den she can find and coming out only to the sound of food.

Sitting on the floor, our kids look at us and mercifully say nothing.

And that's when I think I've understood what has been puzzling me lately. I suddenly feel it all coming together, all the data collected watching individuals wandering this earth without seeming to have a connection, a common understanding, a feeling of belonging to something more than the macrosystem of Federal States, capitalism or the Stars and Stripes.

Over the past few weeks I've been asking myself: "What is it that holds this crowd of individuals together?" Finally, thanks to the neighbors, the cookies, and pulling back from a more demanding exchange, it dawns on me that the answer could actually be really really simple. Because, apart from the designated places and scheduled meeting times, the open secret seems to be that they are all here together, so that they can all be on their own.

Maybe it's my own fault if I see things this way. Maybe I'm still too high strung because of the cyclone and my roots are still hanging in the air, dripping droplets of another country.

But then I remember arriving in Syria, where everything really was exotic and foreign. Where the light and the smells and even the air's consistency seemed to come from a truly different and unknown dimension.

I think back to my house with no roof and our neighbors' balconies strewn with carpets hung out to air. The strong food smells, the pollution, the muezzin's heart-wrenching voice. The dust from the streets flowing up my nose with the smell of jasmine. The smiles, the pleasure in meeting a stranger, the fear of the police. The amenable shopkeepers dressed in long garb. The veiled women looking at my hair and sighing "Haram!" (sacrilege!) as I walked into the market. The Hezbollah barracks I passed every day on my way to the playground with my girls. The young men standing guard on the doorstep with machine guns, weighing more than their years, strapped to their necks. The *mukhabarat* deliberately dressed in dark clothes so that every citizen knew he was being spied on, at every street corner. The donkeys trotting down the streets, the smell of kebab trickling out of stores, the freshly baked bread cooling on car hoods…

And I reminisce how, from the start, I'd felt enlaced in the texture, swathed in invisible fibers; the fibers of languages, habits and duties that string people together. The pattern of their movements, of their relationships, was so obvious that when you saw them you could believe you were looking at a living traditional carpet. It was so straightforward, you knew what people were thinking even when they didn't say a word. And you knew where your place was within that thick and complex composition: you always knew where you stood in the tapestry and which stance others saw you in.

Here in the States, there are millions of threads. Each one with a different color, dialect, intonation and praying position. Threads which have flown here, from distant times and places, to settle in the land of freedom; or were forced here, from far away lands, to safeguard the freedom of others.

And now, these threads drift, each one for itself, carried by the wind of its own circumstances, the choices it has made. They flutter in the breeze and get caught up; sometimes intersecting other threads before continuing along their windy journeys. So assorted, diverse and free, they can never really fill the enormous web they move around in. The web of the Federal States, of capitalism, of Stars and Stripes that intentionally remains wide enough to allow the wind and the threads to continue blowing through, free.

Far away

Our new home is coming together and being filled. It's starting to look like us, reminding us of who we were and what we used to do.

We're all feeling more comfortable, more settled. Recapturing our simple little habits actually allows our bodies to take a breather; being able to sleep between these fabrics, comb our hair with the teeth of that comb, listen to music being played by that machine in particular…

The kids are relieved and take heart. My husband goes ahead assuredly in his bold discoveries. The cat stretches out on the old blanket.

I, instead, start along a slow, foggy slide that I have been through in the past. Sensations become murky, feelings rarified, everything standing at a distance.

The presence of streets and people in the streets doesn't elude me; I hear the steps and the voices, watch the colors and the routes. But everything is opaque as if it were all taking place behind a cold, damp mist.

The meaning of things floats around, lost behind something I can't pinpoint. And I'm surprised others actually manage to catch on, perceive things as existent and alive, next to them, guiding them, walking them through life as if they were wandering through a well known, well kept park.

I, instead, find myself in a dark wood, among blurred shapes, lost in a confusion which can't even be defined suffering.

I've been here before, I know it happens sometimes: it's the alienation that sets in with every relocation. Nothing to worry about. I get through the first heroic period: dealing with all the matters of primary importance such as a roof over our head, a school for the kids, transportation, food and medicine. Then, having fixed this and that, I find myself slightly anesthetized. It's happened before. I know I'll get over it, eventually. The anesthetic will be digested and disappear, and I'll get my energy and my sensations back again. I just need a bit more time. I know that too.

But it's unfortunate because, in the meantime, I find myself experiencing some interesting events.
Like the dinner with some former members of Congress, important entrepreneurs and clever guys who raise money to finance election campaigns.
Interesting matters such as the midterm elections are discussed that night. Will the President obtain even just the marginal majority he requires in Congress to carry out his policy reforms? Or will he have to concede to a quashing Republican majority and abandon the needy to their fate?
Or the excellent reasons behind the need for an organization to protect Italian products abroad whose names are being used to fob off atrocities such as the "True Italian Mozzarella" produced in Wyoming—which can only be sliced with a sharp bread knife.
The opportunity for new ways of developing alternative energy sources in the States, although strong lobbies are opposed. Even the heartfelt attempt at introducing the US to the cheerful, bizarre and liberating Italian carnival: Americans don't have anything like it and we really should pave the way.
I listen, smile and dutifully converse with the guests seated to my right and to my left. But I have the emotional reactivity of an unplugged fridge.

The same thing happens on the other important occasion: the quintessential annual society event which, again this year, lots of swell people attend. Set in the immense dining hall of a luxury hotel, the soirée is dedicated to prestigious Italian Americans: heart surgeons, entrepreneurs, movie stars and Italian special guests, including a famous film producer.
Americans love honoring those who have made it, according

to their standards. They organize loads of events like this, congratulate the winner, whatever field he has distinguished himself in. He is set as an example and celebrated with very long and meticulously planned functions.

At the event for successful Italian Americans, the guests of honor are all on the stage, seated at a very long and richly decorated dining table. The other tables in the immense dining hall are just as richly decorated amid a sea of curtains and clothes, carpets and rugs—all in different shades of cream—and loud voices.

The waiters rush around burdened with vast trays, while loudspeakers call out the names of those on stage and their accomplishments. Then they blare out the speeches of those presenting the guests of honor. Finally they blare out the speeches of the guests of honor.

Meanwhile, videos are being replayed on gigantic screens hung in the far corners of the hall, showing the heart surgeon operating, the entrepreneur doing business, the CEO buying a baseball team.

Here too I feel a bit estranged. Sinking through the confused chatter and waves of color, I feel a bit shipwrecked. I think I'm going to drown.

Strange things happen in this distant, opaque state of perception. Some events suddenly break through, their defined edges so sharp and clearcut they hurt even more.

Like when my husband ran up the stairs of our home and came looking for me while I was taking a shower. With frightened, incredulous eyes, his mouth was repeating the same concept a few times before my brain actually let it sink in.

Our cat is dead.

We went down to get her from the middle of the street, slaughtered by who knows who, at who knows what time of the night, which she always wanted to spend outside, after so many weeks locked up in the small Silver Spring apartment.

The worst thing was neither her deformed shape nor the stiff coldness laying under her coat, normally so soft and welcoming.

The worst thing was the feeling of distraction. How little concern, how little care we'd taken until then of our beloved pet. The fact we hadn't realized how dear she was to us.

Dragged from Africa, where she was born, to Italy and then from Italy to the States. To finally die, run over, just outside our American house, the home we had just settled into.

We live dodging fears. The fear of losing a job, becoming sick, losing children or a friend's affection. We face the fear of growing old and no longer being cherished by someone who once loved us. Of suffering chronic pain or not being able to pay back debts. But we never ever face the fear of losing a cat. Who ever thought of that one?

And this unaccounted pain is a sensation I perceived, loud and clear, for many days thereafter.

I was struck by another flash of sensitivity at the celebration for wounded warriors.

This country is at war. The theaters of war are in Afghanistan and Iraq. You don't think about it, before coming here. But then, living here, reading, hearing and seeing how they insist on their love for the homeland and the good fight, the fight for freedom and the heroism of fallen martyrs, you start to become aware of it all.

Even if they aren't allowed to show the bodies of the dead soldiers on television.

Even when, with so few favorable outcomes, they omit the defeats and underline the objectives.

Even when the rhetoric just becomes a customary refrain, a syrup poured more and more generously over every report.

Despite all this, living here makes you aware of this uniquely American situation, and the fact the United States is constantly having to account for difficult choices, without always managing to justify them.

So they organize innumerable celebrations, commemorations and fundraising events.

I found myself going to one: a classical music concert in honor of war veterans and the wounded. Youngsters of all ages crowded in the large welcoming auditorium set up at the Italian embassy. A bold, modern structure that can be rented for commemorations or social and promotional events. This time it had been leased by a company doing business with the armed forces. Every year they provide wounded veterans with a concert and a buffet and, during the soirée, people donate considerable sums of money to some of the associations helping veterans with their recovery.

"It's a bit like Beretta giving money to the Italian League for Bird Protection," my naughty brain whispered.

But I decided to ignore it. I told myself: "Helping these poor people is really great..." and continued observing.

The wounded veterans huddled into the vast middle of the hall: men and women, alone or accompanied. So many youngsters of all ages all truly mutilated, having lost an arm, a leg or a smile. Their relatives ushering them, pushing their wheelchairs, standing by their sides without crowding them. While the sounds of vibrant speeches about honor and love for the homeland, justice and the fight for freedom, boomed down from the stage.

I listened to the speeches, listened to the concert and served myself at the buffet.

I watched and smiled, shook hands and exchanged greetings.

I noticed some children wandering around the tables looking solemn, wearing ties that were too big for them. They looked like they hadn't foreseen any of this: losing part of a parent to the war. And they hadn't foreseen the parent would lose his memories or the joy in being with them, the will to live, the means to work and provide for their future.

The trenches of loss the war was digging into these children stretched, briefly, inside me, strong and deep. So I left the hall and the celebration. In a spineless hurry, I quickly left behind all that terrible pain.

Out of the dens

Meanwhile it rains and rains. It's raining like we had imagined it would from the plane, when it hadn't started raining yet and we'd already thought "Good grief!"

The wall of sound has encased everything. Even the crickets, which always make a noisy racket around the little houses along the street, are now silent. Those little houses lined up with or without a window on the roof, a white or brown picket fence, porches with or without a swing, entrances with or without columns, flowerbeds with herbs or flowers. Now the crickets are quiet or maybe they are trying to screech out their shrill chirping but no one can hear it because it's lost behind the boisterous wall of rain.

Our little house and the others near us drip and drip, while the bloated streams created by the rain flow down the streets. The tops of chestnut trees and strong, old oaks are bent by thunderous bombshells of water.

Every now and then, a large branch falls. It breaks away with a distinct crack and crashes down onto the dead wood below. We hear it all loud and clear, at night, because there's a forest behind our house and the only sounds that reach us are the rain, the trees creaking and the branches breaking away and falling.

They also fall on the large road nearby, one of the main highways which connect Washington to the cities and states nearby.

We are in a small town called Bethesda, in Maryland. The border with Washington DC is a few kilometers away from our house, but nothing tells you you've crossed it. The same suburban landscape stretches along both sides of it, with the little American houses and all their variations; the parks, the forests of chestnut, oak and fir trees all around.

Very green and sumptuous trees hang over the main roads, their branches woven into the telephone and power lines. Wires that stretch low, along the second floors of the little homes, and are often covered in ivy. Every now and then they are torn down by the wind or the weight of the rain, and collapse with the trees onto the road.

Sometimes the rain dies down and loud drops fall from the trees, down every leaf, the dark, long tree trunks, through the hedges and onto the flowerbeds. Squirrels whirl up and down the trees and dart around looking for food. Crows jump hastily on the grass and woodpeckers scurry along the branches. But these are short pauses, allowing just enough time to look out and realize that the sound from the wall of rain is no longer there. Then the rain picks up and cloaks everything again. Day and night.

By now the air has changed consistency. It has solidified into a semiliquid state which makes us all feel a bit uneasy and in a hurry, as if we were constantly looking forward to something else. In the meantime, we think about the acres of woods our little houses are scattered among and the strong trees that are sucking up all this water. There aren't any puddles or bogs, even after a week of continuous rainfall, even after ten days.

I watch the water cascading, listen to the wall of rain tearing down on everything and, every now and then, I find myself on the lookout for a shadow to stroll along the walls of the house, into the corners and hidden dens, curl up on my lap while I read, or slink through my legs when it's time for food. Neither insistent nor overbearing, just asking to stay, if that's ok.

Because that's what cats do, a friend tells me. And it's true. So quiet and discreet, they blend into the house and almost become its advocate. Creatures made up of imperceptible movements which bring together the hearth and home and nourish them by simply existing.

Then the rain stops.
The sky lifts into a prospect of dizzying blue light. No clouds, mist or limits to the horizon, it rests, clear and sparkling, on the woods and the roofs, the wide roads and blocks of cement.

Everything in the city, suburbs and on the highways is sparkling with light.

The dull green trees give way to the slowing lymph. At night, the first chills drape the leaves and stems, leaving a veil on the lawns which will soon become frost.

As life shuts down, more vibrant and varied tones gradually explode. Surprisingly, within a handful of days, vivid colors are splashed around all over the place. Reds and yellows and greens, initially as faint as they are in spring, veer into aggressive and magnificent oranges, mixed up with everything else down every street.

"It's so beautiful!" I hear myself saying one morning as I watch the sunrise from my window.

I decide to go for a walk and to walk until I tear apart, rip open and break out of the chrysalis which has swathed my senses.

So I put on some comfortable clothes, just like all those who go out in the morning to walk their dogs and their cocoons. I walk, and walk, through the woods, losing myself along the fresh and arduous paths where only the owners of very large dogs wander—to let them run around freely—or some intrepid mountain biker ventures, unafraid of exerting his muscles and running out of breath.

I look at the warm colored leaves shining through the dark branches. I see a rabbit slip away, padding fallen leaves, and a woodpecker persistently poking a tree trunk. I watch squirrels rushing up and down, between the branches, rustling up acorns, filling their mouths and running away towards invisible burrows. Walking among the colors and animals is starting to dispel my numbness.

But seeing things is not enough to spur sensations, we all know that. Even hearing has its limits. The cracking, rustling and wind blowing through the tide of dry leaves can't dig up sensations burrowed deep in the hidden nooks and crannies of our mind.

Whereas smelling can.

Smelling the fragrant mixture of forest and rain, of sunlight drying the carpet of needles and yellow leaves—that's when it happens. When paths rapidly evaporating in the morning sheen overlap with other invisible paths, along displaced axes of unruly memories and juxtapositions.

The parks after the first days of school, the excursions in the Apennines, a lake shore in the company of friends, kisses exchanged on the dry grass of a lawn...

My nose sniffs down the trails of emotions and memories and finally ferrets out those buried sensations. Hidden behind distant thoughts, lost in empty planes or behind drab screens. It flushes them out without frightening them, takes them by the hand, scoots them out of their hideaways and brings them up to the surface. Here, among the colors and the rustling, above the sweet smelling paths, they can finally come out into the open.

Thrill and confusion, surprise and gratitude are set to rights and I feel complete, geared up. So I walk and walk and walk on some more.

I walk until, for the first time, I feel I have actually reached a destination.

CHAPTER II

Long nights

Seasons are steamrolled by cities, flattened out under roads and houses until they all become tasteless and distant.

City dwellers perceive only a mere echo of the Earth's deep, cyclic transformations: outside temperatures shifting, health conditions changing and wardrobes being switched.

Instead, in these residential suburbs, seasons gleam through every window, incorporate you and follow you down every street. Nature changes pace and ta-da, everything changes with it. Schedules, habits and states of mind.

In this part of the world, you really can't miss noticing the colors eating away at the leaves. The American foliage is famous for its very bright yellows, incandescent reds and, most of all, the fluorescent oranges which I don't remember ever seeing in Italy. The foliage stretches over thousands of acres of wild parks, transforming the woodland fleece into a silent explosion of colorful tufts. It also expertly unfolds along residential streets, over rows of hedges and clusters of trees, creating contrasting glowing dyes.

Even when they fall to the ground, these leaves continue shining their colors, warming the streets, now slightly colder, with a welcoming hue.

The only sour note is the new gardening task: we now have to get rid of the leaves more and more often. A few centimeters each day, they very quickly build up into soft carpets. But then decay after each rainfall, develop rot and fungi, create bogs on the door steps and clog the drains. Raking and bagging is a job that doesn't allow for delays or fatigue; it becomes a duty.

Nonetheless, in my heart, I continue blessing all these leaves for the joyful dyes they shed. It's just too bad they vanish earlier and earlier as, at this latitude, the hours of sunlight become shorter by the day.

The darkness is already long, at this time of year, and becomes thicker every day, more complete and triumphant. Like a black tide flowing in, every afternoon, to cover the streets, houses, parks and avenues. Leaving the city to float in the gloom, with only a few lit windows and feeble rings of light from the street lamps—like bits of a shipwreck lost at sea.

The darkness is so thick and long, it's no wonder the grim Halloween festivity was invented. Eerie paper plates and black church candles, skulls stuck on torches, window decorations resembling haunted castles… Objects of the kind start appearing on supermarket shelves, eating away at the shelf space of normal, innocent products.

Devil costumes and full length skeletons, rotting limbs and zombie masks, instead, fill the venues which can be leased for special occasions: clearance sales or sales of products for special festivities such as, in this case, the night of the dead.

Orange pumpkins are piled up into dozens of colorful pyramids inside and outside stores, and create a joyful splash of color in these days full of gloomy shadows.

And we soon see these same objects appearing, in various combinations, in front of all the little houses, scattered on the lawns and hanging from trees.

The large, beautiful, colorful pumpkins—matching the surrounding foliage—pop up on doorsteps, seemingly conscious of the greater destiny that awaits them, announcing something inevitable.

In the upcoming days, before the event, children's playdates are organized, with mothers carefully guiding them in the difficult art of carving. Away with the soft, juicy pulp, so rich in color, and in with the jagged outlines of scary mouths, eyes and noses. A space is cut for a candle to be lit on the haunted night, and the sweet tasting pumpkins are put back in their places, ready to become the repositories—and vessels—of mystery.

On the night in which the dead come back from the afterlife,

I decide I too must make myself worthy of the occasion, so I go up to the attic and pull out an old cloak from a box.

A strange black coat, in fashion in the mid 80s, which I'd kept because it was very long and very warm. It is actually a relic of a slightly confused time in my youth, when I felt both mysterious and in vogue. When I wore black clothes, white make-up and purple lips and hung out in clubs where we pretended to be existentialist vampires.

I put the heavy coat on with a thrill of dark pleasure. Place a witch's hat on my head and go out with the younger kids—dressed up as devils—to scrounge for treats.

We march along in the dark, up and down the residential suburb, walking past homes that are decked up for the occasion.

The pumpkins, now supplied with a burning candle, glow their lopsided sneers on each doorstep. Feeble, creepy lights appear behind the windows, enormous spiderwebs hang on porches while, here and there, ghosts dangle from tree branches, held by invisible strings.

One neighbor even went as far as creating a sort of film set, throwing open his well tended lawn to the disquieting presence of open coffins and skeletons swinging from the branches. With spotlights purposely lighting the props and music sounding through the dark to heighten the feeling of danger and mystery. As well as sounds of creaking, shrieking, and sinister howling.

My kids walk along with the others, in dribs and drabs. Every now and then, they come together along a driveway, rush up some steps and ring a doorbell. They wait patiently, among the symbols of horror, for the owner to open the door and smile, a witch's hat on his head. They repeat the ritual phrase: "Trick or treat?" and, feigning to surrender, he fills their hands or hats with candy, chocolate bars and chewing gum.

All those who have a glowing pumpkin on their doorstep are willing to play the game and stick to the script. Those unwilling don't put up any decorations and are left alone.

We too had got to work, obviously: we decorated our garden with enormous spiderwebs spread over the hedges and crowned them with a giant spider. Placed a dark hunchbacked dummy near the front door, carved out and lit a few pumpkins, then left Dad to welcome kids with a basket full of sweets.

Others created true masterpieces for the occasion. The young couple disguised as pirates, clothed in all possible pirate paraphernalia, for instance, went the whole nine yards and set up a buffet on their front lawn.

My kids dash for the hamburgers generously on offer, while I go for the wine, provided even more aptly. I sip and observe them. So smiling and welcoming, they even dressed the dog up as a pirate: a patch over one eye and a lopsided cape. I wonder what wild fantasies they will get up to once they have kids of their own...

Then we move on, becoming more and more involved in the festivities, behaving exactly like everyone else. Once again mysterious and somehow in sync, like in my *dark* days.

Wandering along in the night when children become Satan's little helpers, I greet the other parents I sometimes meet in the neighborhood. I breathe in the cold, dark air, but also feel a hint of warmth: the relief of actually having a few people to say hello to, although they are hardly recognizable through the shadows, down these streets that are always so silent and empty.

Wrapped in this feeling of kinship, I notice a little blond angel, dressed up as a little blond angel, standing beside me: three years of curls and glowing cheeks. I smile at him and congratulate him for his costume while his proud parents watch over him. Then I allow myself to stroke his head a few times. A few maternal caresses, softened by recent memories. The parents stop smiling, glare at me, grab the child's hand and pull him away.

"You should never, ever, touch a child!" my friend runs up and tells me, her two children dressed as vampires by her side.

I've known this friend for a very long time. Coincidentally, we found ourselves living in the States, in the same city—and actually in the same part of town—at the same time. And every time I see her, I feel heartened. Her children go to the neighborhood school and are invited home by their classmates; other mums contact her to organize parties and playdates. Her neighbors have sometimes invited her to barbecues and she has returned the invitations. Not only does she incorporate a softer and more colorful world than the one I live in, she is also better informed on local customs and traditions. She explains that people who caress children are frowned upon.

"It's considered excessive, too intimate. Even when they fall down and you help them get up again, parents will sometimes be annoyed. You've got to be careful."

I walk along and recall the large mums in Syria, bundled-up in tons of veils, who would grab my little girl from her pram. They would lift her up and hug her, pass her round and smother her with kisses. Because, in that part of the world, that's how children are cuddled and cosseted.

I admit, all that enthusiasm seemed excessive and it embarrassed me sometimes. But I bought into it, accepted it as a different custom, and tried to not show my bewilderment.

"But you were in their Country, not the opposite. Here you have to follow suit."

She's absolutely right. I have to put a stop to my Mediterranean intensity, repress it and stash it away. Or direct it somewhere else.

Dogs are fashionable here. Almost everyone has them and they cosset them as if they were children. Maybe I should learn to do that. I could become like this lady with her kids dressed up as zombies, for instance. She stopped the owner of a labrador to ask him about all the lucky four-legged pet's habits and, in the meantime, she's stroking it, scratching its head and kissing it on the nose. The dog owners are chuffed, smile and proudly answer all her questions. The dog owners' kids standing beside them, dressed up as ghosts, wait in silence, patient and ignored.

"Mum, can we go?"

My kids, instead, are tired of being held back by my thoughts; they nudge me and show me a street we haven't been down yet. So we continue our nocturnal promenade among the skeletons, the howling and the welcoming grandparents answering doors with handfuls of treats. All smiles but no caresses.

When they open their doors, looking through the narrow crack, I manage to catch a glimpse of an entrance hall, part of a sitting room, a few paintings and some of the wall colors. Then the door is closed and, with it, the hope of getting to know someone else's home.

We head back with pockets full of chocolates and candies and the feeling that it was a great party.

As I help the devils out of their capes and tails and free myself of my long coat and mystery, I ask myself why it all felt so enjoyable. What exactly was it that shimmered, with the kids on the front lawns and driveways, in and out of the beams of light shining from the street lamps and open front doors?

Maybe just that: being able to get around freely, in and out of those otherwise impenetrable private properties while, literally, looking like buffoons. The strong and intense taste of freedom, of restrictions and permissions capitulating. The satisfaction of being able to take a peep at the intimacy of these neighbors, who are normally so distant they really do seem mysterious.

And I remembered those who compared the beauty of the Italian carnival to the gloomy Halloween masquerade. Sure, in the States, they don't have the cheerfulness of going out dressed up in broad daylight to make a racket and play pranks. They prefer frolicking with the afterlife and other scary entities at night.

But if carnival is all about knocking down conventional barriers and allowing raids into forbidden territories, then I think Halloween is a carnival in its own right, and among the best of its kind.

Besides, these night time promenades and all their attempts at rebuilding macabre sceneries for the most delicate of us—our kids—to walk through, feel like more than just a game. More like being nuzzled by fears.

Because nights are nibbling slivers of light with every passing day, leaving us more and more at the mercy of everything we can't see. And that's when the Halloween strolls come about, offering a baptism of darkness, to wash away all our worries with some fun.

This intense darkness also brings to mind our arrival in Senegal, at night.

I recall the long flight in the dark. The handful of lights, possibly fishing boats, swaying in an expanse which must have been the sea. Then, the first dim lights appearing on the ground: street lamps lined up on short stretches of road, like small worms of light on the black earth. Lined up at first, the lights then became more frequent, creating whole networks. And finally there they were, the lights of Dakar, appearing in the African night: rows of street lamps that we could count, one by one, as we approached.

It wasn't like the bright cupola which comes to light above European cities, the glow being projected into the night sky, humiliating darkness.

Washington and its surroundings, with long avenues, immense parks and half empty neighborhoods, are also dominated by darkness. It overflows and prevails, harnesses buildings and gobbles up the ends of roads, hiding all perspectives. As you walk or drive along, anything lit jumps out at you, suddenly in close up.

In some way, darkness makes me feel the magnitude of nature. It makes me feel that, to this day, man still can't prevail over the elements. There are such vast open spaces, and the cost of materials is so high, that humans can't even illuminate the capital of the western world completely.

Along these routes, swept by darkness, my mind travels back in time and starts dreaming, imagining the American spaces when they were still completely untouched. Wild, unknown, immense spaces. Plunged, in the winter, in a darkness which those who first arrived had never seen before.

No light, anywhere.

On the immense sea ahead and the immense woods beyond, only some bleak rustling and faint sounds.

They must have been driven by such inconceivable strength and trust to want to face that vast, complete darkness rather than all the problems they had fled. Rather than the lights they had left behind.

Now, called out by darkness, those Pilgrim Fathers reappear in the days leading up to Thanksgiving. Days in which new decorations start surfacing along driveways, above windows and hanging on front doors. Some people still haven't gotten rid of their pumpkins and are already exhibiting large inflated turkeys on their front porches. They look like the inflatable dummies of some rock concert blowing in the wind. But they make no sense whatsoever and really leave me wondering.

Every ad, every radio message, reminds us that we will soon be getting together with our loved ones, and it will be fantastic to think about all the great and wonderful things we enjoy and are thankful for.

This festivity was created by the first pilgrims, apparently. After a long winter of misery and hardship spent in the New World, with scarce provisions, hunger and sickness reducing their ranks, spring had brought the Algonquians and their friendship. From the Indians, they received native seeds to replace those they had brought from Europe, which had turned out to be useless. And they learnt where best to hunt and fish. As well as other ploys such as how to water fields and preserve food.

Autumn then provided a fabulous harvest and the pilgrims' houses were filled with provisions for the winter.

So the good pilgrims decided to celebrate and, being the devout believers they were, they gathered around a table to thank the Lord for all that bounty. They had also invited their native friends who contributed to the banquet with venison and strange animals which turned out to be more than edible: turkeys.

Native Americans and pilgrims feasted together for three days and three nights. This was the first Thanksgiving.

A unique moment, still pure, a beginning.

A time in which people, dressed in black clothes and bonnets, deer skins and feathers, boots or moccasins, beards, braids, glasses or face paints, could still understand one another well enough to talk, without uttering a word, about compassion and gratitude.

A precious time, to this day, in America, when everyone stops and thinks about what they are thankful for in their lives.

I like the idea of a whole country looking within, examining its life to find something good.

As the autumn makes one wish for some warmth, there's a sense of relief in looking for gratitude. It makes one poke around and stoke memories. And find, buried under the ashes, sparks of joy flaring up again. Specks of wonder. Warm ashes of gratitude.

So, to best commemorate this time—which I happily take to—I invite a couple who have just arrived in town. Their paths are similar to mine. Young children, busy days, eyes open on the outlook for something.

Then, faced with the smallest turkey I could find (although still too big to fit in the fridge so it spent days outside, displayed on the garden table, waiting to be sacrificed), the red wine and the joyful sounds of the kids, we observe one another at length. Our families mirroring one another. While we chat about this and that, a warm lightness swells over us.

Meanwhile, all around, families are getting together and greeting guests. After intense discussions about timetables and routes, exchanging recipes and traveling across entire states, now come the hugs, the gifts, the celebrations. Our neighborhood is full of cars coming and going, lights being turned on, the elderly bearing presents, young parents holding the hands of their skipping kids. In the houses and on the doorsteps, everyone is receiving and opening their arms, welcoming and celebrating.

In our house, the husband of the couple we invited takes a pause, ponders and makes a proposition: "Let's stop a moment and think about all the good things we have."

Then, as we aren't good protestants, we give thanks our own way: we raise our glasses and smile upon our lives.

A warm Christmas

After Thanksgiving, we start feeling the first stings of winter cold. A few sparse splashes of snow whiten the roofs, roads, bare branches and the few hedges that are still green. Not a great deal of snow—within a few hours, all that is left are a few long ribbons along some edges. They remind me of the light striations that appear on overexposed photographs.

Nonetheless, while the terse air creeps up my nose, my brain is numbed with visions of dens, of peace, fireplaces and easy times.

Nights freeze up and, in the morning, the frozen snow shines, dangerously, on steps and curves, along the roads up and down the city. Meanwhile the darkness extends even further and cradles wishes for soft emotions to snuggle up to: getting away from these cold grasps, unknown faces and the silence of this neighborhood. Leaving this new life, just for a bit, and go back to feeling some warmth, all around…

All of a sudden, this thought becomes a desire, and soon after an urgent necessity. As natural an instinct as breathing and, like my breath, I can no longer hold it back.

I want to go back, just briefly, to the warm certainties we came from.

So we fly through the turbulence and the frost of the northern hemisphere. Airports going crazy, exhausted travelers and relatives waiting at the other end, babbling Hail Marys. We travel through the ups and downs of our stomachs, jammed in narrow bus-like seats, on an eight hour non-stop flight. And we are finally back in our sky, our airport, our country.

Even the faces of the ground staff tell us we are back. As well as the cleaners and the cashier of the café where we order our first meal, at seven o'clock in the morning. The taste of that first breakfast slots into our deep memory, and suddenly everything feels ok, normal, easy.

On Christmas Eve, we find ourselves at a family banquet and I feel as if I've ended up in an Italian Commedia dell'Arte. Not as a spectator but exactly where I want to be: centerstage, surrounded by masked actors following my cues.

A reassuring comedy in which I know all the characters one by one and expect to find them exactly as they are, as they have always been, stuck in their roles. We know all the previous acts and can guess what the script has in store for the next scene. We deliver our lines, each pulling and being pulled by invisible threads, safely juggling our moods, knowing all too well what effect our words will have.

I flutter about in a kind of euphoria and can't stop smiling and greeting everyone.

"You've made it? It's so great to see you... and not for a funeral, for once!"

Some sneer, others glare. But I go on laughing, chatting and hugging because I'm exactly where I want to be: in a turmoil of well-known comedians who make me smile, crack jokes and get emotional.

Then I look around and recognize my eyes, my smile, someone moving their elbows the same way I move them. Mirrored here and there, I see an explosion of genetic history and similar habits.

We all come from far back, with this mishmash that is our essence. So many centuries and ancestors, so many encounters and fortuitous combinations have brought us here, to mingle and show off our latest offspring: new children who have just the same ears as his dad, the same way with words as auntie, that cousin's skin color, "No, he looks just like his great grandfather!" and so on.

They've all been in my life for so long, these relatives, all around and below, protecting me like a solid safety net I could land on in case I fell. They've always been there, even when everything else didn't always feel safe.

An American doctor once told me about a medical study that was carried out many years ago in a small town with a strong community of Italian immigrants, all very closely-knit. They studied these immigrants over a number of years because they realized they were less likely to become sick; they lived longer and were healthier than other American citizens. But the scientific study hadn't revealed any genetic mystery or predisposition for better health.

The immigrants ate the same food as everyone else, had the same physical structure but, still, they were healthier and lived longer... Why was it? The same study then outlined that the strong relationships, the help they gave one another, the fact they all knew they would never be on their own, throughout their lives, were these immigrants' prerogatives. Therefore the only plausible explanation for their good health was the solidarity they all showed towards one another.

As I fly back, in the vast darkness of the sky, I think about that medical study and how emotional the American doctor became when he told me about it. He was one of those many people in the States whose faces light up when you talk to them about Italy, and they smile as if they've recognized something good and healthy. Although they rarely know anything about the real Italy and confuse history and geography in a mishmash of information containing only a few certain facts, one conviction remains unshakable: Italy is beautiful.

So, thinking back to the doctor's dreamy smile, I'm reminded of the fatigue and the extra effort which people in the United States have always faced in the absence of a safety net. Families dissolve like sugar in water once kids have left school. One here, the other there, all looking for the best life they can find. These solitary paths are the norm. Each one for himself: taking on debts, risking, losing and falling, or doing well and making it to the top. Like a mountain climber or a solo navigator. Knowing there is nothing between himself and catastrophe.

So that brings me back to Thanksgiving, and I now see it all from a different angle. A rare moment in which we aren't only moved by the wonderful things we have. The idea of getting together and having fun resurfaces. We seek one another out, crossing from one ocean to the other to shake hands, just for one day. To make our presence felt and realize others are there too; while everything else swiftly tumbles away, we still hold hands, smile and carry on.

Different times

Once the holidays are over, everyday life picks up momentum, gets back into motion, then accelerates and finally sets itself to a regular, steady pace. School days are set out according to fixed commitments, work goes back to its challenging rhythm.

All is well and back to normal.

Now even the garden is sleeping. The last time I tried digging a shovel into the ground, the metal blade was bent and the kickback made my arms vibrate painfully. The ground has been frozen since before the first snowfall and there is no point in trying to get anything done.

So I decide to take the time to observe. Until now, things have come to me and I could feel them suddenly hitting me. Bewildering, painful or pleasant, but always in a sudden wave that would surge, cover everything and flow away again.

Now, instead, everything out there is lying around me, in plain sight.

And I start wondering exactly that: what does and doesn't this country allow itself the time for?

First of all, there's a time for greetings.

Everyone here, and it really is everyone, takes the time to say hello. Whenever neighbors run into one another, strangers meet, the postman delivers a parcel, whenever the instructor walks into the gym, the policeman asks you to open your bag in a museum, or the cashier starts scanning the groceries...

But they only take the time to ask how you're doing, and maybe add a smile. They've greeted you, made you feel more at ease. And that's it. No wasting time, once they've taken the time to say hello.

They say this direct and offhand approach dates back centuries. To the times when the pilgrims landed here, in the vast uncontaminated nature. They came, full of courage and trust, and sank into the wide open spaces and the long winter nights. Whether in small groups, or on their own, human contact was inevitably rare and precious.

The rite of kindness towards strangers is typical in extreme places. We experienced it even in the Syrian deserts where the more isolated tents, of those nomads who had never seen a European in their lifetime, were the first to be opened and reveal smiles, bows, carpets, tea in tin cups and goat milk treats.

Whether in a forest, a desert or a frozen expanse, how can one not welcome other human beings? Their life depends upon it. The meaning of one's existence, for each and every one of us on this earth, depends upon it.

I imagine a woman dressed in long thick skirts, a bonnet on her head, wrapped in a shawl; her husband wearing a dark, rough coat, long sideburns and a wide-brimmed hat. I see them on their wagon, bouncing along with every irregular bump on the almost invisible path through a dark overgrown woodland. They advance slowly in the cold, their hands, full of calluses and worries, gripping the wooden sideboards and reins.

They reach a cabin made of wooden boards and beams with a wagon similar to their own standing by and a fenced enclosure for the animals. A wisp of smoke blowing out of the chimney.

The woman and her husband smile, silently; they have reached their new neighbors. It has taken them all morning but they will soon be safe and warm.

In the cabin made of boards and beams, a woman dressed in heavy clothes is stirring up the fire in the fireplace. Her hands, rough and aware, move from one to the other of the few objects in her possession. With a strong grasp, she holds the cooking pot, the poker, the fan blowing air into the fire, the cot with a crying newborn child.

She is startled by the sound of a wagon approaching.

"John…?"

But it can't be her husband: he went behind the cabin an hour ago to chop wood and the air is still being filled with the sound of the sharp blows breaking the logs in half, and then again, and again.

The woman puts the poker down and straightens her apron, picks up her shawl and wraps it around her head. She hears that her husband outside has stopped the sharp blows to the wood and is walking up to the road.

"Oh God, is it really happening?"

She runs to the door, grabs the handle and rushes out to see who is coming up the drive. She hasn't seen anyone in months.

As soon as the two couples spot one another, they wave and smile even if they are too far away to actually see each others' faces. As soon as they are close enough to hear one another, they call out "How are you?" and "Welcome!" "So nice to see you!"

As soon as they reach one another, they shake hands, and forearms. They tie the horses and go straight inside the cabin.

"Did it take you long?" "Where have you come from?" "Are

you hungry?" the couple ask as they open the door to their warm room and gesture their guests to the fireplace. The new neighbors extend a basket full of food.

"We have brought you some things you may be needing."

And then, as the years go by, from one generation to the next, I can see a series of isolated cabins, arrivals, greetings. I can see a long trail of encounters and handshakes, waving and calling out.

Blood bonds and history—winter after winter, encounter after encounter—bring us to nowadays and today's average American, who walks out of his front door and nods to his neighbor or calls out "Take care!" to a passerby while getting into his car. He smiles hello when he gets to work and starts his day by saying "Good morning!" to his first caller.

I try imagining this average modern American in Italy. The company he works for has sent him to Rome. Or Florence. Or Milan. Or wherever the company has sent him.

He gets to the building where a flat has been rented for him and as he walks up the stairs (because the company has chosen an attractive building, close to work, in the historical centre where buildings are tall and narrow and don't have an elevator), he feels he's been a bit unlucky. At the airport, the attendants seemed bothered. "Who knows? Maybe the last trade union request didn't get accepted." And the taxi driver who brought him into town had been so brusque—"He must be ending his shift." The passerby who bumped into everyone without even bothering to turn around was probably busy with some difficult task. The newsagent who sold him a guide was probably annoyed with the umpteenth foreigner asking for the umpteenth guide. "I've been a bit unlucky," he thinks. "No one has said hello to me."

And as he is thinking all this, he walks up the stairs with his heavy suitcase and heavy omens which he tries to drive off as if they were bats flying around a few centimeters from his head.

He gets to his landing and tries to find the right key in the St. Peter's bundle he was given by the real estate agency. He rattles, chooses, tries and eventually finds the right key. He is about to open the door and enter the flat that will be his home for the next few years, when the door on the other side of the landing opens and out comes a tiny old lady, shoulders stooped and handbag held tightly to her chest. The American smiles at her immediately, showing all his shiny white teeth: "Buongiorno!"

The little old lady is startled and tightens her grasp on her handbag. She's about to utter a slightly surprised complaint but decides to hold it back. Meanwhile she stares at the keys in the foreigner's hands and the open door of the flat opposite her own.

She thinks "No, he's not a thief," while staring at him and checking him out. Within a handful of seconds, she gauges a series of factors she has been taught to appraise by her Italic ancestors ever since her early childhood, passed down from generation to generation, forever in her family history, during the war years and pre-war years of both world wars, and further back over the centuries, to the Unification of Italy, the foreign invasions and the Middle Ages, back as far as the Roman Empire and earlier still, when they were divided up into small goat-owning villages, since the beginning of time, when they lived in caves and fed on berries.

You have to think so much before allowing anyone to approach: is he stronger than you, slier than you, does he come from a powerful family, a family opposing your own, from a hostile country, from a foreign culture, is he carrying a weapon, is he a loafer? And finally: what does he want from you? Some information, a favor, a loan, a declaration of intent, a political belief, a religious abjuration, an indecent proposal, moral support...

So, head bowed, the old lady leaves him standing there for quite some time while her bony knuckles grasp her handbag; she leaves him standing there, his smile slowly closing, his teeth losing their shine. Until the American feels the need to explain himself because he realizes that, in this country, a smile is not enough. He comes closer, offers his hand and says: "I'm your new neighbor, I'm American, here for work, and I'll be staying a few years."

The old lady sizes him up again, this time faster and more serenely. She sorts the information, takes into account the various possibilities then finally smiles and shakes his hand: "Piacere!"

Maybe, at that point, she grips him in her gaze and holds him tightly between her wrinkled eyelids. Finally smiling and with a profusion of questions, offers, chit chat and warnings, the American starts sweating and regretting the detached silence that falls, among his countrymen, after the affable: "How goes it?"

He opens the door with his foot and starts pushing his luggage inside, while the old lady continues chatting about a distant relative who lives in Chicago; he falls back, without letting her notice, while she asks him if he's married; he manages to half-close the door while the neighbor offers to supply salt should he ever forget to buy some, and eventually he closes the door on some complaint about being old, how lonely it gets and that she has no one to talk to.

Meanwhile, back in the American's homeland, someone takes the time to notice all the things that people take the time to do in this part of the world.

They take the time to write up a bill and get it wrong. Then ask you where you come from while writing the bill up again.

The time to fill the shopping bags with calm, wise gestures while you, the spoiled customer, await in a peaceful limbo.

The time to let pedestrians cross the road, to yield at a crossing and leave you the last parking spot.

The time to insert the wrong information into the computer file then laugh about it, say sorry and peacefully start all over again. Meanwhile smiling, and asking you where you bought those cute glasses.

The time to take a child by the hand, look him in the eye and explain why he shouldn't lie to the teacher, he shouldn't get angry if another child gets better results, he should share his games with his friends. And why he feels frustrated he can't have a puppy now instead of next Christmas.

Where I come from, a Mediterranean scolding would suddenly erupt, whereas here, they take the time to kneel down and talk. Sometimes with harsh, authoritarian words, but at least they talk. And I think back to all the times I snorted and pulled away, snorted and slapped, snorted and yelled that I was sick and tired.

Above all, in this part of America, they take the time to run and run and run some more, at all times of day, every day of the year. To stay in shape with small steps, little jumps, short strides, simple ambling or long steps. Each person chooses his pace depending on his age; wearing dazzling sports gear or plain clothes.

The old man with white hair stays fit, his memories strolling along in front of him as he walks down the path in the park. The lady with coiffed hair and her dog wrapped in a cape. The girl with earphones and a high-tech running suit. The boy with a headband, his body steaming in the freezing cold.

Instead, I'm always either in pain or fighting the first symptoms of a cold. Or the tail end of a cold. A past trauma to my joints flaring up again. A bad day, an errand, someone to see, stiffness in my bones, the waning moon... So I watch them admiringly, running and jumping, as if they were all tougher than me; aliens from a distant galaxy who have landed on Earth to flaunt a prodigy: one can actually have a life and find the time to keep fit.

In general, people here take the time to do things. Without getting het up, feeling guilty or anxious. Just doing what it takes! No one scoffs at someone taking the time to do whatever. And everyone takes the time to show respect.

Sometimes I'm the one getting antsy and restless and feeling guilty—all at the same time. Haven't they got anything else to do? Haven't they got somewhere they need to be, some urgent matter to deal with, the feeling they have something better or more important to get on with rather than what that guy there is doing, just taking his time?

Then I realize I'm the one who is off kilter. I spin around dizzily and just want to toss away everything around me, hurl to the side all the obstacles laying on my path.

Hurry up, do it well, time is money, you snooze you lose, first come first served and *mors tua vita mea*[2].

Maybe I've lived too long in Italy, in cities where crossing the road was a life threatening luxury. And now, here in America, I rush across the pedestrian crossing to not annoy the driver who has stopped to let me pass. While others around me take their time to walk across, and the driver in the car takes the time to let them.

I end my short run, put my foot safely down on the sidewalk and turn around to look at the other pedestrians walking along, wrapped up in their winter coats, eyes down and time on their side. And I realize how much time I waste by doing things in such a hurry.

When I lived in countries where globalization hasn't crushed, ground and spat absolutely everything out again and shreds of other civilizations and economies still survive, I would stupidly rank the efficiency of different cultures on a scale of speed. How long does it take to get a certificate, for a utility to be connected, a letter to reach its destination or an outage to be repaired.

And while I doggedly interpreted my surroundings according to my personal criteria, the world around me wouldn't give a damn about this or that and went about its business in its own time.

The African village women walk along slowly, glancing at things, letting their gaze wander. A child tied to their back and a heavy bucket of water on their head. They walk along slowly, standing straight and don't seem to have a worry in the world or any burden awaiting them.

These women make you wonder how one could live walking slowly along, taking the time to look at things, without worrying about what the future has in store.

And watching them, their slow glances and their steps willing to accept things as they are, one can't help asking oneself why we are no longer like that. We were in times past, for sure, when women carried baskets on their heads and sang while going down to the river. When the world was made up of villages and fields, hoes, wagons and horses and there weren't any clocks.

So? Why exchange this for that? Why torture ourselves with rebellions and illusions such as youthfulness, fitness and wealth? Why don't we walk like that any longer: one step after another, looking ahead instead of forward?

I'm well acquainted with a girl from Senegal. She comes from one of those peaceful villages, marked by strong sunlight and shadows, distinct sounds, voices, wind and red sand. Women forever tying children to their backs, men forever bent over hard clumps of earth. The river flowing nearby and mangroves with roots rummaging through cloudy water.

This young girl came to the States to work, among the stressed and pale white people who take their time at pedestrian crossings, sure, but spend their lives running after a thousand different things.

Full of fears and regrets, the weird white people who always want to know what is happening and why. And how to make it happen again, if they like it, or not happen again if it is not to their liking. Who worry about the illnesses that linger treacherously in the city air or which their own spiteful bodies decide to invent to make them suffer, become ugly and die.

Intolerance, discontent, the ground slipping from under their feet… and the white people believing they can do something about it. Trying to stop time, create extensions, safety jackets, bridges… how weird.

How can she manage, having come from a land of slow strides and wandering gazes? Having lived with the peaceful wind blowing through baobabs. And why? What has she exchanged her plight for? For the salary the white people give her, "for peanuts," as someone used to sing, "and this asshole's glory."[3]

She'll go back to her village in a few years' time, covered in glory. Full of experiences which her people, among the baobabs, have only ever heard of by word of mouth, at night, under the infinite stars of the African sky.

With stories about white people having this and that. Large houses where they live alone. Cars, and lots of them—each person his own—which they drive around in even to places they could reach on foot. They have television, several televisions, one in each room so that they can each watch it on their own. They have computers and radios, machines to wash clothes and machines to wash dishes. They have medicines and lots of doctors, and hospitals as big as cities where they take you when you get sick and you leave having been cured. They have money, more and more money and they don't share it with anyone because they are selfish and mean. They have as much food as they want, and more. So much food they have to watch out and go on diets. They have food at home and in restaurants, bars, shops and in the streets. Food from everywhere in the world, even African food, which overflows from their bodies; oozes out as sweat when they run and run to work it off. That much food.

The people from Africa with their hard skins, skinny bodies and long muscles taut in the wind shining with sunlight. The sand covering their pores and veiling their hair. Fine, airy sand that nestles under their eyelashes and in their clothes, as if it were the talcum powder of the poor.

Why do they leave, why come here?

Why does mankind always pursue the mysterious mirage that makes him strive, work, become overwhelmed by expectations and fears in order to grow, become resourceful and transform what he has around him?

Misgivings, spaces, mysteries. A skip and jump, and let's move on. But there is always another obstacle up the road, so why even try?

Why don't we stop? Why don't we just listen to time go by, to the voices, the wind blowing and only that, the blood pulsing, for as long as it's pulsing. Gazing, advancing slowly, looking at what is ahead…?

And yet.

No one has ever stopped. No one has ever sat down beside the obstacle. No one is ever happy with just wandering around the world at a slow pace, looking around. Not even the women from the Senegalese villages, when they can get away. If they are given the chance, they take off to become stressed and fat among the pale faced men.

"They've been brainwashed," decrees a man I know. "Americans and white westerners in general have imposed their systems, they've destroyed ancient cultures and disrupted the mindset of entire populations."

His sentencing perplexes me. Is it really someone's fault in this case? Can you really tell someone to make do, let himself go astray, not foresee what he is bound to need next or not prepare for future dangers?

Is the human struggling for opportunities really a cruel consequence of consumerism? Or, rather, an inescapable instinct?

It evokes in me an image: affluence as the desirable nipple of a distracted and elusive sow which all of us unweaned piglets try to grab with our senseless, hopeless, heart-wrenching need for life.

The snow has come and gone

We awaited it for so long; got ready months in advance, we and the whole of Washington, for this great event which can be very annoying and sometimes catastrophic. Heaps of it on doorsteps, blocked roads, difficulties in getting provisions, treacherous ice, broken bones and blue noses.

So we read the street signs to understand where we should and shouldn't park the car, in case of a snowfall. Because whole streets must be cleared, down the side, to make room for the heaps made by the snowplows. And we read the school instructions on what to do and who to contact in case of bad weather, because, here, everything, absolutely everything, closes when it snows. It only takes a few inches and everyone stays home: all school kids and all the employees in all the public administration offices. The radio, television and major internet sites spread the news. I truly think it's a good idea. Why don't we do the same in Italy? Why complain about traffic jams, accidents and delays? When it snows, stay home! Then plow and spread salt on the main arteries and secondary roads—forgetting about the smaller streets—and there you have it. No swearing and less damage. And all that's left are weird cars with large plows on their front fenders squeezing out of garages and getting to work down the smaller streets—which have been abandoned to their destinies—to clear them and connect them to snowless roads.

Having gained all the information, we bought shovels of all sizes. The biggest for dad, a smaller one for mum and the smallest one possible for the only one of the three kids who may want to lend a hand, just for once.

Well-equipped, feeling a bit like the family of bears in Goldilocks, we awaited. Wood piled in the garage and food reserves in the basement.

"We were stuck at home for three days last year," some old-timers told us. "Actually four."

So I added some cans of peeled tomatoes to our reserves, and pasta and frozen grated parmesan. God forbid we run out of spaghetti for three whole days...

We already had snow boots and thermal underwear. Hats left over from skiing holidays as well as gloves and thick socks. We'd started using them even before the snow fell, of course. Because, with delicate Mediterranean zephyrs in our chromosomes, we lost all semblance of normality as soon as the temperature fell below zero: snow or no snow we just had to dress up like the characters in an Italian Advertising Council ad for flu prevention.

We weren't the only ones, by far. The wonderful thing about this place is that you are never the only one. Any idea how many immigrants there are from much warmer countries? How many people don't care a damn about the way they look? And the number of hypochondriacs there are out there? Plenty.

So, here, we find ourselves among people wearing fur hats, others with Peruvian hats that hang down over their cheeks or the latest high-tech outfits against the cold. And we never feel strange. Not even when we come across rare specimens in long sleeved shirts. They're out there too. Although the ones we see are our German neighbors, with their pale faces, who stoically cope with the cold.

Equipped for the outdoors, with a feeling we are to experience an epiphany, we settle in to await for the big event.

The temperature drops, and drops again. The cold breeze cuts at our throats, freezes the tears in our eyes and the air in our noses. We breathe sharp scales of wind and wait.

The trees have no memory of their leaves. They just stand, naked and spent, throwing their branches towards the grey sky. They are obviously asleep. And everything that used to scatter around them is also sleeping. The woodpeckers and cuckoo birds have disappeared, whereas the squirrels, rabbits and foxes are hardly visible, hidden behind hurried dashes.

There's a great deal of silence around the tree trunks now that the decomposed leaves have been absorbed by the earth and become a hard surface which no longer muffles our footsteps.

The little houses seem to have also become quiet. As though the doors and windows have now lost the voice they had not that long ago. The gardens seem to have taken off completely, as though their joyful spirits had migrated god knows where and left behind their bare remains, burnt by the frost.

Even the sky seems to have something better to do. Low, bloated clouds silently roll by towards other destinations.

Then, one evening, as we return home from our various activities, we are greeted by a strange light, fanning out everywhere. The sky is even lower and more radiant than usual; almost like fog, thick and boundless, resting on trees and houses. It reverberates, prolonging the twilight. The silence is thick, the cold is almost pleasant.

"It's going to snow tomorrow," I declare to my kids, my nose sniffing the air. "Or maybe even tonight…"

We become emotional, speechless, as we enter our home in awe.

And, that night, a few small, fast snowflakes start to sprinkle down. But within a few hours it turns out it's just a blast of ice raining down from the sky, whitening a few patches here and there, nothing more. Disappointed faces, the school opening late and traffic jams, that's all. With ice triumphantly taking over the driveways, steps and sidewalks and pouring out of gutters. Sneering, treacherously, where you least expect it and making your bum hit the ground when, for just a second, you forget it's there.

We all feel a bit let down by this short snowfall. Two, three lousy sprinkles that are just a nuisance. "Just like in Italy!" we tell ourselves, a bit disappointed. We put the shovels away and sulk.

One evening, finally, the usual sprinkling doesn't stop soon after starting. It continues, insistently, pricking the ground with needles which become whiter and whiter, larger and larger, and slower than before. Then the snow stops falling and starts flowing down softly. It wraps around itself, spinning and whirling under the garden lights and street lamps.

"Maybe tonight's the night," I declare.

A few minutes later, our front garden has vanished, as has the road between the houses and the pathway down from our front door. The driveway to the garage has also gone.

I pull out the mum sized shovel again, bundle up more than James Cook in the North Pole and spend a good hour and a half freeing the access to the garage for when daddy bear gets back from work.

At five o'clock in the morning, the school is declared closed. I look out the window and see snow piled up on the terrace railing, two hands high. And it is still snowing as though it had only just started. I snuggle under the blankets with a shiver and a satisfied smile.

That night is followed by days of pure joy watching the surrounding white world while the silence echoes in my ears and the sky is sometimes white, other times blue. The snow rests idly in the dark or sparkles when the sun shines down—the houses, cars, gardens, buildings and trees all under a pure, uniform blanket. All differences are cancelled, everything is cancelled. All there is left to do is walk through this layer of equality; sink your feet into it and feel the weight crunching down and crushing it.

And watch the kids' satisfaction, overjoyed in their warm beds knowing that what was meant to be a day spent sitting behind a school desk will instead be a day at home, doing only what they want to do; with, possibly, a few friends over to spend the long dark afternoon hours together. I relish their happiness and joyfully start writing, in the silence of my room while outside, in the dark, the pure, even coating grants a feeling of peace and warmth to our home.

"What?!?"
"Haven't you had a blackout too?"
Our friends' voices shudder, unbelieving. So I check it out and discover from the newspapers that while we were enjoying the peaceful warmth of long dark afternoons, whole neighborhoods in Washington and the suburbs had been without electricity, heating or hot water. Camping around their fireplaces, whole families had been left to shiver and become enraged with the power company who had abandoned them to their destiny.

It's all about those wires hanging low between the branches of the trees again. A gust of wind, an intense storm or a slightly heavier snowfall is enough to tear them away from the poles and throw them to the ground. Followed by traffic jams, colds, children home from school tucked up by the fireplace like modern little match girls.

We, instead, warm, well-fed and content, go to buy a set of sleds. Different sized sleds because, by now, we like pretending we are the bear family.

And down we go on the slopes behind our house, our cheeks quickly filling with cold air and freezing sprays of snow—tumbling, panting, shrieking and jesting.

"Come ooonnn, let's see who gets there first!"

Then up, weakened by laughs, as our steps sink our way back to the top. We bend over, push one another, yelling and screaming our way back up with our breaths failing, loudly happy.

Eventually I look around and watch the other children from the neighborhood. They are poised as they slide down the incline, then stand up, grab the cord and patiently start up the hill, their sleds following them with a gentle rustling sound.

We, the typical loud-mouthed Italians, have made the windows of all the nearby houses tremble with our terrific shrieking.

Maybe I should intervene and impose a bit more restraint, Hey! Do we always have to make ourselves known? Then my little one challenges me and darts down.

"Hey whimp, catch me if you can!"

I jump on my sled, push off with my hands and throw myself after him, down the incline, with a very long scream.

A few days later, it's all over.

It has rained a bit. A frozen rain which hasn't melted the snow but hasn't built it up either. Just created pockets of ice in the streets' dark corners.

Then the sun comes out and the temperature rises. And the snow starts melting and loses its uniform coating over everything. Everything becomes what it was before, as in Cinderella's fairy tale. Everything goes back to normal, nothing is hidden any longer, nothing is the same as everything else any more.

The roads are all roads again—curbs, gardens, bare hedges, benches, grey shrubs and abandoned swings blowing in the wind; the kids go back to school, everyone's electricity is on again.

Days grow longer, afternoons are veined with more and more light now. A little more each day.

It's an odd sensation, this wintery world lit by long afternoons of light. There is no sign of spring, yet, just more light illuminating dead nature. The same grey trunks. Same branches reaching up to the sky. Same spent colors of the leaves on the evergreen trees.

While merciless light reveals and scans it all. Pointing out the stones covered in moss, frozen trickles of water, piles of blackened snow, blades of grass burnt by the frost.

I, too, find myself a bit naked now that the snow has gone. In our empty house and the silent gardens. Working, with no epiphanies in me, and walking, with no cries of joy.

The snow has come and gone, and I feel exposed again: myself, in full light.

CHAPTER III

Slow awakenings

Spring brews slowly in this part of the world. An extra minute each day, a fraction of a degree, a bud on a bare branch, a green blade in the yellow grass. The rich, warm humors are still hidden inside the plants and animals.

Everything moves slowly.

The squirrels scamper around shyly on the hard ground. The lethargic rabbits jump in air which is still cool.

No smells, hardly any sounds.

Everything is potential. It's still invisible but already out there, somewhere, coming back to life one little bit at a time. Existent and non-existent at the same time. Still hidden away in the bare tree trunks, spring is an opportunity that will certainly come to life.

On the first calendar days of spring, with stiff joints and no muscle tone, I lazily reach the car and open the door. I'm neither a badger nor a dormouse, but I too have been hibernating through a sort of shut-eye winter, in lower gear. My thoughts, vapors exhausting from my brain, are just as slow.

The birds are chirping, jumping around, happy in the few, fleeting, rays of sunlight. I start the car and realize I could have gone on foot, after all. It's Spring! A bit of exercise would do me good...

Instead, staying below the speed limit, I squint, dreamily, at the world outside.

I watch the slow dragging along of this invisible, barely palpable, transformation. Just like in the autumn, when the never ending spread of colors through nature took place. But, at the time, we could still enjoy the remains of summer's glories. It was a graceful, sweet, slowing down which prepared you for the worst with hardly any suffering. Now, instead, the dribbles of a cold, dark season don't seem to want to let go of their landmarks.

The fascinating candor and danger of the snow have gone, leaving behind a grey, heavy, end of season cloak which is slowly exiting stage right.

In my cold driver seat, even after all these months driving automatic, my hand is still looking for the gear shift and my foot revs up the engine in neutral.

Italy comes to mind. A whiff of warm wind carrying a sudden, languid scent, full of moist, sweet smells. The swallows flying over and shrieking, every nest an explosion of chirping. Buds sprouting and opening, colors and smells spilling down from the trees and up through the hedges.

Here, in Maryland, I wonder whether I shouldn't put some heating on in the car. Then I decide not to, I haven't got far to go. I turn on the radio, instead, and let the exotic sounds of American ads strike my ears. Full of long sounds and blasts, laughter, slang and a firing out of short words I don't understand.

By now, in Italy, days are long and the light is strong. A light which warms the skin and slides into its pores, sparking sudden ideas. Intense desires for something else, something new and unforeseen, flourish and go beyond usual sensations. Wishes so strong and eccentric they could be considered bothersome.

And everyone starts complaining about the sudden heat, as well as the sweaty, sleepless nights and daylight saving upsetting everyone's moods.

Oh, the Italians are master complainers. About everything, absolutely everything. It's not a real protest; how can anyone protest against nature? It's more like a natural—almost inborn—statement of the fact one is alive and thereby destined to a subtle, permanent, unhappiness; the feeling that you've been cheated, and your wishes have been neglected by the world.

What do Italians actually expect? A continuously soft summer, velvety chirping breeze and perfect sun rays at all times of the year? And surprises, stimuli, eternal hunting and eternally new prey, unknown suns and double moons, new faces on the bodies of old lovers?

Surely, between one complaint and another, everyone has hormones skipping around inside, dazzling them with indecent thoughts. We look, smell, walk with livelier eyes and rounder hips. Our skins, still white, shine through clothes that are suddenly lighter.

Here too some people go around in T-shirts. Our German neighbors are the first. Off they go, their pale skins on show and their expression hardened, as always, by sheer willpower. At seven thirty in the morning, we still enjoy being wrapped up beyond reason, as usual, while the low blowing winds bite away at every uncovered morsel of skin.

Our noses and cheeks turn red and we sneer, spitefully, wondering how we would be suffering if we were standing on the street dressed like them. Short, sly remarks made by people who have nothing else to do, at seven thirty in the morning, while waiting for the yellow school bus.

Each school has its own bus stop and they're all lined up near one another. So children and parents wait, watching the slow, steady traffic flowing along in the same direction. In the evening, it will flow again, in the opposite direction.

At that time of day, the only things out there are the boring, slow, lanes of traffic and the wind nipping at every inch of unprotected skin. So even the slightly blue faces of the German neighbors become a funny distraction.

Now, instead, it's afternoon, the light is clear and hesitant signs of spring are breaking through. But still neither scents, nor whirring or buzzing. A sterile spring.

What with these buds hanging, here and there, from bare branches, I feel like I'm in an eighteenth century Japanese painting instead of an East Coast street in the early afternoon.

The yellow bus rounds a curve in the distance and comes slowly along the lane. It draws near, turns on its roof light, pulls-up to the sidewalk and opens its doors.

One at a time, three sets of legs disembark, three faces hit by the sudden light. Then three tired heads saunter, slightly stooped, towards the car.

I try to find my voice, after the long silent solitary hours, and greet them. I smile, grab a backpack, deliver a kiss. My questions are followed by strained answers, emerging from after school numbness. Then I get back behind the wheel and fall silent. Respectful of their fatigue, I give in to my own.

As I'm driving along, I look out again at nature struggling with its moult.

"Mum, my friends in school say God exists. Is it true?"

Slow spring and difficult questions...

Again my hand's on the inexistent gear stick and the engine isn't in line with my feet.

Habits and thoughts just as inadequate at supplying answers.

"Look, my love, there's a squirrel!"

"Even Paolo, in Rome, said God exists, and that if he behaved badly God would know and punish him."

"Punish him?"

"Yes."

Some mothers never get tired. They don't have slow springs and their minds never grow sluggish. They have ready answers, prepped in advance.

And the nerve to shove even more fears into the minds of the innocent, as if life itself weren't already full of them.

"You see... I... believe God exists, in some form. So, for instance, numbers exist, right?"

"Yes.»

"But it's not as if there's a *mister one*, a *baby two* or stuff of the kind, right? They're ideas... they exist but they aren't really there, they're abstract."

"And God?"

"It's like numbers... our way of identifying aspects of our lives and the universe. In other words, God is the name we give to the mystery behind the creation of the Earth, nature, and humankind. And before that, the energy which made galaxies and stars evolve. We call all this God."

It's more or less the third time that this mum finds herself confusing her children's minds. More or less at the same age each time, asking the same questions and with the same expression on their faces. Kids are consistent. They ask about sex at one age, death at another and God at yet another.

It's the third time she sees her child glaring at a senseless knot of words, and getting upset because his mum doesn't hand it to him straight, like Paolo's mum. God exists. He sees and judges you. Like some sort of grumpy granddad who may even whack your shins with a stick every now and then.

My mother always had a gloomy vision of God. A weird, sadistic guy, according to her, who invented a universe based on cruelty. Nature, as some sort of enormous life-grinder, forever mixing itself up while pounding human flesh, animals, plants and minerals in an eternal triumph of death and destruction.

My mother didn't complain about the seasons, but she did complain about God. Her observations erupted in floods of protest and discontent; a sort of register of grievances where she listed all the inequities God caused with his careless, blind domination. Listening to my mum, you would almost think the loathsome tyrant should be ousted with a revolution.

Having witnessed my mum tormenting herself all through her life over the sufferings we humans had to endure, I thought about her point of view over and over again, and finally decided her explanation was not acceptable. I came up with a less painful one of my own in which the above mentioned mechanism was not put together by some perverse mind, rather by an irreversible, unavoidable, incomprehensible energy mystery we can't escape. Because we are up to our necks in it.

"Actually, we too are God."

There, the final jab.

Usually, the child now squints at me and doesn't return my hesitant smile.

This youngest one instead is capable of focusing his mind on what interests him most, and everything he sees or hears, that doesn't suit his frame of mind, can take a hike. In this case, he must have stopped at the part about the universe and who created the Earth, etc. because he gazes at me, satisfied.

"So God is much more magical than Santa!"

I laugh and sigh with relief. It was so simple after all, why make it so complicated?

"Of course! A whole lot more!"

If I had a fourth child, I wouldn't be caught off guard.

"Mum, does God exist?"

"Of course he does, my love. He's like Father Christmas, but so, so much more magical, and he created everything, the world, animals and people!"

And I would leave it at that, hoping a few more years go by before the eternal game of asking "why?" kicks in. That unrelenting, ruthless chain along which kids hurry down, hopping from one link to the next, urging you on to give a meaning, connected to another meaning, in a dizzying sequence. And quickly reach the point where, I believe, even Paolo's mum would start having doubts.

In the meantime, we have reached our cute American house. I pull up to our front lawn and park the car. As I'm turning off the engine, my youngest has already jumped out and started running up the path, his schoolbag bumping against his legs.

And God has suddenly become an odd, likable guy who gushes out from all corners of the universe, warps and expands, explodes, squirts out, calcifies, crystallizes, dies and turns back into himself again.

He sprouts on branches, gushes out in birds' songs, lies down on the grass burnt by frost, jumps up and down with his schoolbag bumping against his legs.

He closes the car door with a soft thud, and opens the front door with a casual sigh.

A matter of style

Once inside, I delete my thoughts and make myself a coffee. I wait, with that mix of impatience and drowsiness I always get while the coffee is reluctantly seeping through the moka pot. I'm watching the brown bubbles of foam spurting out of the metal spout, when I suddenly hear a loud racket that makes me jump. It sounds like a body has just decided to land itself in my front hall. Then comes the sound of a metal object slamming.

I turn off the stove and sigh. I could be living in the States for decades and still jump every time the mail gets delivered!

I pour the coffee into a cup and go to the front door, my thoughts moistened by the sharp smell of the hot drink.

And there, fanned out on the floor, is the pile of letters, brochures, coupons and ads the postman has just put through the flap. I scoop it up, skillfully balancing cup and papers, and take it to the kitchen. Then sit down, sip a bit of coffee, sigh and start; the mail ritual must be tackled at least once a day otherwise it stacks up so high I can no longer bear facing it.

So. A few bills (they are sent once a month, here, with a return envelope to mail back a cheque written up with the amount owed), various subscriptions addressed to the previous tenants who—the wife being American—had subscribed to a remarkable number of things: theaters, auction houses, mail order catalogues for clothes, mail order catalogues for homeware, magazines for gardening, cars, furniture, Easter decorations and Christmas presents.

I make a pile of all this essential correspondence, ready for pulping. Now for the ads.

Flier after flier after flier with offers for teams of industrious Peruvian maids who'll clean your house with a smile (they call themselves the "Merry Maids"), expert gardeners who'll turn your garden into Versailles, competent chimney sweeps with brooms of absolutely inconceivable sizes, genuine Neapolitan pizza makers who make pizza with garlic and ketchup just like in Italy, cobblers, nearby laundromats, plumbers and framers. I make a second pile, drink a bit of coffee and continue.

Coupons. A stash that's delivered oh so often, which I can't bring myself to throw out just like that because, once, I actually used the one from a boiler maintenance company and they gave me a discount.

My survival instinct forced me, at least once in my American life, to have the enormous boiler checked. It takes up a whole room in the basement of the house. Night and day, it puffs away and trembles, lighting up and turning off with sudden blasts of pipes, cogs, valves and mysterious mechanisms which I'm never happy to go near. Do come and check the Moloch I keep in my basement!

And I ended up paying through my nose for them to tell me that it was just fine.

I knew the discount was already included in the bill, obviously. All the boiler maintenance companies put their prices up then hand out coupons, you just have to tow the line. So I gave the cash and the coupon to the workman, closed the basement door behind me and, for once, peacefully ignored the pistoning and banging produced by the machine, behind my back, saluting me farewell. They said it was just fine, after all.

So, I sift through the new pile of coupons to discover what I already knew: I didn't need anything.

I resist the temptation of signing up for a qigong course with a fifty dollar discount for the first month, and start yet another pile. I finish my coffee and look at the remains of this mail orgy which I'm always a bit dazed and surprised by. Why the blitz? What is it with the constant spilling over of paper and fliers, magazines and leaflets on the floor? Why this obsession with wanting to reach into my most intimate space and break my sacred right to be left in peace, with all these offers?

"Sure, but there aren't any poster ads in the streets, here."

My eldest daughter points out.

I think about it and she's right. That's what was missing. That's why the sidewalks, the highways and the lanes of asphalt in the suburbs are so squeaky clean.

No billboards, or signs, or even posters stuck to the walls. Absolutely none.

"It's the same in Washington; haven't you noticed?"

My daughter adds. And I admit it's true, there aren't any ads in the streets there either.

"I always used to know what films were showing. Now I have to look them up on the internet."

Exactly, that's the difference. In Italy, we walk around and are told, every step of the way, about the latest film, the latest perfume, the latest sale.

You become knowledgeable by just walking to the baker and back.

Here, knowledge must be acquired through an initiation rite, in the intimacy of your private space, opening envelopes and reading in thoughtful silence. Of course. It fits. Dealing with ads within one's domestic realm suits this place and these people's disposition. With somewhat understated messages, directly from the supplier to the customer, and slogans that are almost childish when compared to our very colorful billboards. The "Merry Maids," so cute.

Here, you can quickly get used to the calm language and forget the constant Italian shrill.

The subdued tones had surprised me when, at the end of October, we had gone, as a family, to a big rally.

It was called: "Rally to Restore Sanity." Super.

Thousands and thousands of people marched across the Mall, in the heart of the capital. Precisely along the space filled with vast lawns and trees between Capitol Hill and the Lincoln Memorial where, some forty years ago, youngsters had marched against the war in Vietnam.

The place where Martin Luther King Jr. had broadcast his dreams to the crowds.

The same space, often seen in documentaries, packed with crowds of hippies and inspired faces, fierce-looking policemen on horseback, posters, raised arms and clapping.

I was wandering around, blissfully energized, feeling like I was part of something important and ritualistic. Looking at people's faces, finding their eyes, smiling. I would have liked to talk to everybody and say: "You're right, we're right. Enough with all the stupid exaggerations, guys! Let's yell it out!"

But then I realized that the exact opposite was taking place all around me: there was no yelling out.

A poster declaring "I left all hyperboles at home" set the tone.

But it wasn't a show of intellectual snobs. There were people in checkered shirts normally worn by loggers, some leftover radicals from the sixties and coiffed ladies. Fathers who had come in from the residential suburbs for the occasion, with healthy faces and a child holding each of their hands. There were some easy riders with leather jackets full of studs and sideburns growing down to their chins. A group of Rasta and another of Hare Krishna. And lots of DC employees who had left their iPads at home, with their hyperboles, wandering around looking pale and convinced, while quietly showing their discontent.

I walked up to a young man with a serious expression and colorful clothes who was watching the crowd, a bicycle leaning against his leg. I asked him who had organized the rally.

"The comedian Jon Stewart talked about it on The Daily Show. Ever heard of him?"

"No, sorry."

"Well, he talked about the idea of giving the moderates a voice because they usually don't have any say. We only ever hear those who yell, who are violent or exaggerate... So he and another famous comedian, Stephen Colbert, decided to bring people together here today. And Oprah Winfrey, you know her, right? Ok, she helped too and it sounds like there are more than 200.000 of us."

"Really?"

"Yeah, and at the show a few hours ago, with the comedians and other guests... It was incredible, I've never seen so many people!"

"But what exactly is this rally protesting against?"

"Against the exaggerated tones being used in the media in general, against the daily distortion of reality. And, above all, against the unacceptable, shameful tones of the latest election campaign."

I nodded, said I was sympathetic and in agreement with the protest, spoke against the heated tones. The cyclist smiled back.

"Unfortunately it's a common evil, not only in the United States... Where are you from?"

I felt like saying "from the North Pole," instead I confessed and muttered that I was from Italy. The guy was kind and just chuckled.

"Well then, you know what I mean."

Then he got on his bike and pedaled away saying "Take it easy!"

I went back to meandering through the peaceful mass of people shuffling along. Many disguised with masks of all kinds and soft slogans against strong slogans.

I could have floated around for hours on end in the sea of protest, tirelessly agreeing, for once, with no reservations.

But the kids were tired, my husband satisfied and my feet out of shape. So I left the wavering, reassuring rally to go home.

On the way back, I was wondering why these good citizens were feeling so indignant. I had the impression everything here ran smoothly, as if it were some sort of catholic girl school, compared to the filthy blaring I was used to in Italy.

Here, where Obama is always President Obama. And anyone mentioned in the press is at least Mr So-and-so. Where, a few days ago, a local newspaper referred to the swear words hurled by an Italian Government Minister at the Honorable Members of Parliament as: "Words which cannot be printed in a newspaper."

Here, where politics certainly include a degree of bribing—but it's all a matter of lobbies and semi-secret agreements, corruption at the highest, almost invisible levels. Where appearances uphold the politeness of civilized living. Where a leading politician, young, ambitious and with a promising career, resigned when a ditched lover posted a picture of him bare-chested on the internet. Nothing more. We, Italians, would almost feel sorry for the poor sucker.

Sadly, the cup is empty. The coffee is gone, I can't count on it to pull me out of my daydreaming. I scoop up the large pile of useless mail and throw it in the recycling bin. The dirty cup goes into the sink and I rinse it. Then, as always, I go back to the bin full of waste paper, open it up again and fish out the bills which I threw out with everything else, by mistake. Sooner or later they'll cut my power.

"Mum, which is the best website for cinemas?"

There are lots of different websites. But only a few cinemas with lots of screens. And an overwhelming smell of popcorn that knocks you out as soon as you walk in. But even more surprising than the very sweet, buttery smell, is the dull programming in American theaters.

American comedies. American blockbusters. American indies. American documentary films. American exposés.

The programming posted on the walls of multiplex theaters is strictly indigenous.

"No, look, there's a French film!" my husband and I once noticed.

We walked up to the poster and saw the film was in fact French. But, surprise surprise, it was about the fate of people in Central America.

"Look, that's a foreign film!"

But the main actor was American.

"What about that one?"

The director.

The story.

The location.

The production.

Basically, there has to be something American otherwise the film isn't released.

Sole exceptions are the films with Oscar nominations or some unavoidable blockbusters.

"All the music here is American too," my husband added.

And that statement, made by a man who is passionate about rhythm'n blues, jazz and rock, got me thinking.

I realized he was right. Everything here is sung in English. Radios play the rock classics I used to consider legendary when I was young which now, being broadcast at all hours of the day and night, have become a bit tedious to my ear. Or dance hits. Or Adele, overflowing from all frequencies.

Just like with films: if you are not American, sound American, have an American name, or at least talk or sing in English, you won't be aired.

"And there aren't any foreign newspapers. They're almost impossible to find. Haven't you noticed?"

"Really?"

"Absolutely."

"In the whole of Washington?"

"And surroundings."

"But it's the capital of the United States. That can't be true!"

The shrugging shoulders said it all. There are no foreign newspapers here, that's the fact.

"Mum, I'm going to see a film with my friends on Saturday; can you take me?"

I reassure my daughter I'll be available and get to work on my computer. But the issue of films, songs and newspapers is still buzzing around in my mind and I suddenly wonder: what about television?

Now in a research frenzy, I leave my desk and park myself in front of the TV set. I'm not an expert, I missed years and years of programming while back home, and haven't changed my habits since arriving here.

But I must investigate, discover; so on goes the remote and I patiently start going through the hundreds of cable channels we have here.

There are reality shows about people buying houses. About women dieting. About policemen chasing thieves. About alcoholics detoxing. About alcoholics getting drunk. About young single mothers. About couples preparing their wedding. About housewives who hate one another.

And TV series about scientifically dissected bodies, mysterious bodies, hospital bodies, tortured bodies, rotting, butchered and mourned bodies.

I tell myself that once I've dealt with this research, I can, after all, go back to missing out on all the great stuff American television has to offer, just like I had missed out on all the wonderful Italian programming for years.

I stay strong and continue zapping.

There are TV series about adolescent friends, adult friends, only African American friends, only white friends. And those about angels, ghosts, aliens, perceptions, visions, premonitions and out of body experiences.

And then finally! The foreign TV series.

Stuff in Spanish, South American soap operas with faded colors and stiff actors talking for long minutes about great passions, without ever moving a finger.

Hmmmm, I wonder. This programming isn't all that foreign: the hispanics are, by now, the largest minority, the community with the highest number of kids; some even say they are the future of the United States.

Finally, I go back to a reassuringly black screen, convinced even that box has nothing non-American to offer.

Then I ask myself why. There must be a reason, it can't be just a coincidence, an oversight or evidence of superficiality.

Why is everything American in America?

Then, I hear myself again and the question extends to a new level: what is "American?"

Is it Native American, African American, Hispanic American, Italian American, Jewish, Arab, Indian, wasp…?

"I'm American!" is pronounced with so many various accents and sometimes it's so tinted with intonations from other parts of the world, which have nothing to do with America, you can hardly understand what the person is saying.

But the speaker's eyes tell you that he feels American, and he is.

Ever since he got his social security number, opened a bank account and started paying taxes. No one has helped him and he hasn't bothered anyone. He works and goes ahead and buys his house and his car and goes on holiday and spends time with his friends. He can look at the person asking where he comes from and, barely managing to overcome his Urdu, Azerbaijani or Swahili, firmly answer: "I'm American!"

It's a simple social agreement, here: all you have to do is work, earn, buy, respect the law and pay taxes. No one bothers you, no one helps you. That's all it takes to be a fully-fledged member of this society: no one will question it; not even those who boast about having a pilgrim father ancestor can deny your citizenship. And you'll easily be able to declare yourself part of this community.

I think that's what it's all about. You can feel like a citizen of the place whose rules you have accepted. And if there are so few, inclusive and clear-cut rules, it's no surprise they welcome people from so many different places.

"What bothers me is that in my country, they are changing the rules as we speak," I confess to an acquaintance, some time later. "It's no longer what I signed up for. Sure, ups and downs, dark times and mysteries have always been part of the game. But now things are different."

"You think so?"

"Yes, they are for me. Now I feel lost."

The acquaintance looks at me, bewildered. He's not sure. He feels politics have always been this way, low and treacherous.

"Maybe, but politics used to stick to some rules, right? Playing foul, but within certain boundaries, and knowing where we came from, what we had fought against to create a society we considered better. Knowing what kept us together, really. I mean, anti-fascism, the unity of the country, the sanctity of democratic institutions, guaranteeing a welfare state... But now? What does being Italian mean to us, now?"

The person I'm talking to smiles mockingly. Craftily winking at some recent erotic-heroic exploits by some members of our Government. I sigh. Lately, it seems pointless to even talk about these matters.

After lunch, my family and I leave. On foot, because the acquaintance we were visiting lives near our house.

Once outside, my head still spinning with thoughts about my, our, national identity, I trip on a bump in the road and fall.

My husband lends me his hand.

"Look how ruined these streets are!" he observes as I'm getting up, and we all agree.

We expected them to be even and well-kept, before we got here, with the latest skid-proof technology and perfect guardrails and numerous, rational street signs. Instead, in the residential areas, we walk down streets with no sidewalks, full of potholes and power lines swinging from tree branches.

"Talking about trees, didn't I tell you? My colleague's roof was destroyed by a branch falling from his neighbor's tree."

"Really?"

"And they won't even pay for the damage."

"What do you mean: they won't pay for the damage?"

Apparently, here, things of the kind are considered an Act of God and too bad for you. The government isn't liable. Nor is the neighbor who's been saving money by cutting back on pruning.

God wanted it that way.

Even my mother would be surprised by how the Almighty, here, can be blamed for absolutely anything.

But no one complains.

Everyone here is very patient with God and the public administration. In Italy, for instance, no one would put up with a crossing like this one, where a four lane road cuts through a park and unlucky pedestrians are knocked down every so often. When it happens, several ambulances are sent out, sometimes even firemen with shiny red trucks. The police signal that some half dead guy is laying there so drivers give him a wide berth, take a quick look, then move on. There are hardly any signs and no street lamps. In the daytime, pedestrians look out cautiously; at night, they wear fluorescent gear. They don't take any other countermeasures. Or take anyone to task.

Meanwhile, past potholes and dangerous crossings, we reach our own streets.

A friend of ours, jokingly, calls this neighborhood "The Land of the Hobbits". Our neighborhood. And the name fits perfectly in this season. Freshly mowed lawns and hedges covered with tender buds and the strong light intensifying the cleanliness of walls, roofs and driveways.

Because the roads full of potholes belong to the county, whereas houses are privately owned and very well kept.

People are like that, here: they want fewer taxes so that they can spend their money the way they want. And they love putting money into real estate. They cover themselves in debts to have the biggest and most beautiful house possible. While often still paying back student loans. Americans live laden in debts, but pay lower taxes.

They could also lose their job from one day to the next because there's no job security.

So, finding themselves full of debts, they take out more loans, end up in jail or under a bridge. From Hobbit Land to the land of sorrows in a wink.

Spending so much money takes a lot of courage—courage in choosing loans over taxes and freedom over peace of mind.

Walking among the clean and tidy little houses, we've reached our own home. I like it, that's for sure. But... would I land myself in debt to have it? Would I converge all my daily exertions and risks on it? Would I mortgage my future and the future of my family to own it?

I've always had a reasonable imagination and my wishes usually come once opportunities have already passed. I tote around such unrealistic dreams that I have never actually taken more level-headed ones into consideration.

No, I wouldn't burden myself in debts. I'd rather live with whatever I could afford with my income; four walls, so long as they are secured. And I wouldn't get a degree if it meant being weighed down throughout my adult life.

Ever since a friend's son told me: "The problem is I got a degree because I wanted a good job but, now that I've graduated, I have to take any job I can to pay back my student loan," I'm surprised normal kids, who don't come from a super rich family, even go to university.

But, as I said before, I'm not inclined to gigantic efforts. If someone else, in my family, hadn't planned and fulfilled a career, I would have continued depending on opportunities and chance encounters. Happy to be working among people by day and leaving problems behind at night. Without that hotbed of determination which makes people burn all their resources in the furnace of a single project.

Transformations and actions

As time goes by, days become longer, houses open up and become full of light. There are a lot more people in the streets and parks, waving hello. Peruvian babysitters taking kids out to play, mothers jogging along with their prams, enslaved dog owners being dragged around by their pets on leashes of all styles and lengths.

Meanwhile I feel I have lost something.

Estrangement is no longer threaded into my fibers. No longer a filigree for my thoughts and perceptions, it no longer filters every single moment of my days.

I don't know how or when, but it too was working silently all through the winter. Its humors have ripened, changed consistency inside me, and now I have shed it, like a snake sheds its skin. It remains close by and I can feel the chill it secretes, but it's allowing me to look around and be distracted. I can forget about it, more and more often, and actually bring myself to greet a neighbor or a street corner I now recognize.

As the days go by, the sky soaks up all the air and moulds it into a blue so blue and clear it seems solid. The birds in the woods aren't shy any longer and mix calls and chirps, shrieks and flights, all through the day. They wake me at sunrise, but that doesn't bother me any longer. I lay still and listen, surprised by how noisy Peaceful Nature can get at the break of dawn.

Gardens are embroidered with more and more colorful flower beds. In front of every house, the hedges which I'd mourned as twigs dried out by frost have transformed — like princesses going to a ball — and are now flourishing with pink, fuchsia, white and yellow flowers. The weeping willows are spilling down their delicate buds to the ground, the plum trees are sprouting their lavish petals up to the sky.

The vegetation has really and truly prevailed over the death imposed by frost. It stands there, gorging with warmth, pollen and light, pleased with its own colors and smells.

It feels like the fulfillment of the ritual which had started in March with the cherry blossom. The cherries had been the first to make it through, awaken and spit life out of their dark branches. Like proud messengers, with their bright white corolla budding through the grey dryness, they had borne the good news here and there: to the suburbs, the parks and a few lucky streets in the city.

Then they received the collective visit, the pilgrimage, of those paying tribute to their strength. All the inhabitants of the city and nearby towns flocked to the Potomac river and the alleys nearby, where the cherry trees are most numerous.

These cherry trees had been donated by the Japanese, one hundred years ago, as a friendly gesture. The Americans appreciated this plant and had started using it to decorate the banks of the Potomac. At the turn of the 20th century, the Japanese brought three thousand little trees and another three thousand in the Sixties, creating long cherry rows.

We all know the Japanese are the masters of color and gardens. And with their gift, they brushed this corner of the West with beauty.

Every year, bewildered families and kids, singles, young friends and elderly couples, hold hands as they congregate under the bright, white flowers and the blue sky, and smile. They take pictures and look around in disbelief, suddenly feeling lighthearted.

People need to share this special moment when we all feel freer and lighter. We need to meet, look one another in the eye, walk along rubbing shoulders and hips, saying sorry, I didn't mean to step on your foot... And allowing the kids to bump into us, agreeing to take group photos and have others take some for us.

The tall, smiling sky casts upon us, small warm-blooded creatures, lost among white petals, its benevolent yet haughty glance. Sometimes puffing a gust of cold wind to warn us: "Watch out, I still have some left in me!"

In fact, there has been a lot of rain and storms, drizzles and still more rain. The Southern states have had a series of tornadoes throughout April and May, razing thousands of houses to the ground and wiping out hundreds of lives.

Mississippi. Alabama. Missouri. Oklahoma. The same dull grey skies, the same dismayed people, transfixed, looking out over the disaster. The pictures in the newspapers show empty expanses, flattened landscapes with a few wooden boards piling up here and there and junk lying around; a gigantic abandoned yard instead of a city.

The President gave a speech. The President visited a disaster area. The President promised the Federal Government would send aid.

I see the President's face more and more often, and he looks thinner and more drained than ever before. As if this young, self-restrained President were being sucked in by his office. It may sound stupid to feel sorry for him. After all, this tall, thin gent is the leader of the most powerful country in the world. At his age, he's already had the most unexpected, sudden, fast and enviable career. How can one feel sorry for him?!

But I still think he looks lost amid all the troubles raining down on him.

Except on one occasion.

As he's about to start a press conference, on May 1st, his eyes are shining with satisfaction. He has something up his sleeve, I can see it a mile away.

And that's when he announces that a few hours earlier, in total secrecy, a secret commando completed a very secret operation which had secretly been in the making for years.

Osama Bin Laden is dead. "Justice has been done."

The President's satisfaction is understandable: at a time like this, the financial crisis, his enemies attacking him viciously, a drop in the poles, natural disasters… what could have been more appropriate? I'm happy for him and I'm pleased to know Bin Laden is no longer out there wreaking havoc.

But I'm still surprised. My eyes watching the screen and my mind lost in images of biblical justice. Eyes taken in exchange for other eyes, teeth jumping out of gums and landing in the dust with other teeth.

Because, in my mind, the word "justice" steps forward stiff, formal, severe, dressed in a cap and gown, full of pretentious exchanges. Loaded with documents and law books, thousand year-old ethical questions and regulations, precedents, courtrooms…

Whereas the killing of Bin Laden, and whoever else was nearby at the time, hits like lighting, fearless. It jumps down swiftly from a helicopter and strikes vengeance, bang!

But it seems to worry only me and a handful of others. I realize this a few hours after the news breaks, when thousands of Americans pour out into the streets—all of Washington's streets—rejoicing, jumping up and down, showing banners and signs of victory. They look proud, triumphant. They have evened the score.

I would rather have seen Osama humiliated by the law, beaten by the superiority of a system which solves conflicts with rules instead of terror. Seen him fade away and disappear behind bars.

I'm uncomfortable with the idea of someone landing anywhere in the world, just like that, from another country. Barging into someone's house and killing four or five people, plus a well-known terrorist fugitive, then jumping back into a helicopter and going home to celebrate, triumphantly.

I must be a sad, depressed mental case. I can't bring myself to joyfully cry out, or get my cords to vibrate in unison with those of the country I'm now living in.

And I have to be careful now, because of all the glorious light and green everywhere, and what feels like a big amusement park starting up again. Sadness could turn into something sweet and heart-wrenching, and slide into the folds of spring, like a soft place you would never want to leave.

I really miss the swallows. Their high-pitched voices chirping about unknown events from faraway places and joyful adventures. They arrive from sheer, brightly lit places, where light and wind meet and every amusement is allowed, every sensation free, easy and endless.

CHAPTER IV

Plucked cleaned and content

I wonder how Americans find their way round the dark forest of private companies that make up the health system here. How do they garner the optimism and inner strength they need to get hold of healthcare?

By comparison, I come from a little vegetable garden. A small, safe, fenced off plot the stork chose to leave me in when I was born. There, I grew up, became an adult and chose my path. A small vegetable patch, with a few potholes and dark corners you could get stuck in. But you know it's going to be ok because you can always count on it being there, and no one will ever kick you out. Sometimes you curse it, often bad mouth it, but in the end, you always take it for granted.

Here, instead…

"What insurance do you have?" the doctor's secretary asks me off-hand.

My answer will determine the quality and quantity of health care I receive. My future hangs in the balance.

I hesitate as I hand over a card with all my insurance information. And while I wait for the young lady to photocopy it and insert the data into the system, my mind takes off.

I have just handed over the card of an insurance that will only cover a small number of bills because my present employer is unwilling to pay for a better one. I'm an average American, still paying back my student loan plus the installments for my house and my car.

I'd be better off having no income whatsoever right now or being a jobless single mother with four children, like those who get away with basic, free health-care. OK, it wouldn't be great but it would still be better than nothing. Instead I'm an employee with a fixed salary so if I get ill I have to pay, and through the nose. Also, I'm still better off than my husband since his employer hasn't given him any health care at all.

I've used up all my savings for the kids' education. My illness could make us bankrupt. And there was no point in trying to renegotiate my health insurance, looking through the small print, applying to the local free health care programs, appealing for help from a support group, getting assigned a voluntary consultant. Nothing: the treatments are too expensive.

I'm behind with the car payments and, if I go ahead, I could lose my home. How am I going to pay for all this? And, if I don't pay, well, I'll just die.

"Here you go, thank you," the secretary wakes me and hands back the card.

I take it and sigh with relief: I have good health insurance, so if my condition turns out to be serious, I'll be able to get treatment without going bankrupt.

I thank the secretary profusely, as she throws me a weird look without saying a word, and sit down to wait my turn. I pick up one of the usual magazines about how to stay fit, thin and beautiful and not end up in a doctor's office for a medical exam, spend money and go bankrupt.

I had never fully grasped the importance of prevention before coming to the States.

Anyway, even with good health insurance, things aren't that easy: "If you have a decent health plan, they prescribe you a lot more tests," I've been told more than once.

I turn the colorful pages, trying to ignore the faint tension that always vibrates through the air of a doctor's office, and the reason why I'm here. But instead of being distracted, I can't stop thinking about the stories I've read or my friends' warnings:

"Those who can pay for doctors are like hens with golden eggs in this country!"

"In this country, you're never healed; they want to cure you for the rest of your life!"

Meanwhile the page in front of me with a beautiful American street and a beautiful American woman in her garden, explaining how grateful she is to the doctor who diagnosed her Restless Leg Syndrome, transforms under my eyes. It becomes larger and more complex, full of objects and animals: a farm.

On the farm, well insured citizens, with little round eyes, skip around fluttering their golden feathers. Meanwhile creepy guys in white coats stare at them from their hideouts. Every now and then a white coat catches one of the citizens and squeezes him until he poops an egg, and another, and another. He's cackling away that he isn't ill, he's feeling just fine. But the doctor hangs him over a big pot of boiling water (the dangers of becoming sick) and tells him he will end up in there if he doesn't get treated. So the sucker is so frightened he spews out more golden eggs and lets the doctor pluck him clean.

The other citizens, with lousy insurance policies, stand there without reacting. Some of them aren't feeling well and try attracting the attention of the white coats. But all their bleating, braying and oinking is useless: they are just common animals, beasts of burden that become useless once they are ill.

I put down the magazine because there's no point in trying to read. The farm has also disappeared, but my mind is still churning. I think about President Obama who felt this system wasn't all that fair. He and his supporters had tried to argue that all those golden eggs could have been put to better use. If the finances of the American economy stopped flowing into the hands of those farm doctors and their skyrocketing bills (which are covered by insurance companies!), maybe the hens would be able to invest in the stock market or start a company, take a holiday, buy a house… And the farm could grow and become more beautiful, better kept and more comfortable. Maybe some lame horse or sterile rabbit could even be treated with a few of those golden eggs.

And he added that bosses should be forced to take out health insurance for the animals working for them because it isn't fair otherwise, they shouldn't be abandoned to their own devices when they become ill and be made to lick their wounds themselves.

Instead it didn't work out. The lobbies stepped in. Shifted the power this way and that, fudged, dodged, spent lots of money and got away with almost everything they wanted.

Also, when Republicans are asked to regulate anything dealing with society at large, they become furiously scornful and react as though someone were asking them to kill newborn babies.

On this particular occasion, they argued that poor, sick people are bums and there's no need to help them. And if the President made citizens take out insurance, gave health plans to those who couldn't afford them before, forced companies to take on sick clients as well as healthy ones and coerced employers to supply their employees with health coverage, it would be an outright intrusion on people's lives. Like forcing all Americans to eat broccoli.

That's what they said.

Besides, I didn't need all these fussy arguments. I was annoyed by this system as soon as I arrived. So I'd turned my little bald head, spread my wings over my chicks and hidden behind a barrel, hoping the white coats wouldn't notice us.

I'd managed to stay hidden for several months. But then, hearing them yak on about the dangers we all carry around inside ourselves, I started having doubts: do we all go around like unconcerned idiots with no idea as to the nuclear time bomb we have in our bodies?

The pediatrician here had given me a serious look while his assistant nodded in agreement to everything he was saying, and I became more and more frightened. He felt my kids could have all sorts of problems, including health issues I'd never heard of before, such as lead poisoning.

"Lead poisoning?"

The assistant nodded again while the pediatrician explained:

"Water pipes here are very old and could contaminate the tap water, there have been several cases already."

And he pulled out old health issues relating to my kids and turned them into new problems. Because no one had taken any notice in the past, whereas now, this pediatrician—with his yes, Sir assistant—was making a big deal out of them all.

It had taken weeks of check-ups and turmoil, worries, tests and bills (even good insurances don't cover all the expenses) to get to the truth: the kids were actually as healthy as we had always known them to be.

At this point, the rooster husband had rebelled:

"You see? I told you there was nothing to worry about. All that anxiety for nothing... Enough, from now on, no more talking about doctors and tests!"

He'd jumped onto a barrel and started pecking at all the white coats trying to accost him.

"Jump up!" he'd said. "Don't let them catch you!"

Instead, I, the meek brooding hen, handed myself over to the doctors and signed up for all the check-ups.

Had I known better, I too would have jumped up on the barrel.

Instead, I let myself be overwhelmed by tests, and found myself hurled through alarm bells.

In the past, life had plunged me into specific, sudden unexpected events: accidents, my organism sometimes misfiring, and urgent hospitalizations... Sudden, unforeseeable throes of pain that didn't include fear. Just instinct and immediate reaction, no time for anything else. Sure, I'd had to lick my wounds afterwards, but I knew where I stood and what the consequences were.

This time, instead, I can see danger coming for me from a distance, I have time to assess it, scrutinize it properly. And I decide I really don't want to rub shoulders with it.

For the first time in my life, I'm afraid I could actually be sick.

Now, living here, my fearful state of mind swells up, stretches out and invades the whole stage. I can't dilute it by asking for further information, the advice of professionals or even the simple compassion of my loved ones.

When the danger of a possible illness lands, it takes over. Talking to me in a foreign language about menaces I can't recognize, and situations I don't understand. Then, bluntly, handing me papers that whisper something worrying and unclear.

I feel I'm in danger and I feel stupid, because I still haven't understood exactly what degree of trouble I find myself in. Of all the dangers I've been told about, the only thing I've understood is that, as of now, I am fully qualified for cancer prevention because I may even have some in me.

And now that I am actually living in fear of an illness, I find myself far from home. The place where my tissues feel connected and moist, where affinities, energy and humors hold me together and keep me going, is over there, on the other side of the ocean. My here and now, instead, is isolated and aseptic. And my tissues have been torn from where they belong, and have ended up in some lab somewhere.

I feel alone and sterile as I wander around trying to make some sense of it all.

Like an explorer landing in a new world, I discover a reality made up of customs I'd never dealt with before. Such as doctors supplying lots of information, in their blunt, detached manner. They tell you everything, then let you decide. But if you mention the fact you would gladly listen to their advice, you see them clam up like an oyster, their pearly knowledge tucked neatly inside. They risk being sued if they dare give you an illusion or unclear explanations, so they just hand over the data they have put together and it's up to you to decide.

So I find myself going down a slippery slope, strewn with thousands of expert opinions, and they are all extremely expert in this part of the world. I sometimes feel I'm part of a joke: so, there's a guy who knows how to write and a guy who knows how to read. Because for every specialist in Italy, here you often get two. Duplicating testing times, waiting times, bills, and inflicting long, exhausting journeys...

"The doctor will see you now."

Finally. I can put an end to the memories, observations, and comparisons between the two health systems. I grab my stuff in a hurry and follow the assistant grinning the tense smile of someone working for a doctor who can't afford to waste any time.

And he doesn't waste time with useless smiles and goes straight to the point. And, as I expected, he doesn't have an opinion. As always, just the bare facts and a short speech:

"It could be serious. We'll need to do more tests. You'll have to have a second operation, more invasive than the previous one."

I walk out of the doctor's office.

Walk out of the elevator. The lobby. The building.

A new energy has sparked up in the last few days. Now that the fine season is settling in, the strong light is spreading through the air, no longer recoiling from the overbearing winter darkness. It has prevailed and now reveals everything in a slightly exalted fashion: the office buildings and residential buildings, the shop windows of the mall, the very long roads, the flow of cars and strolling pedestrians. Everything nicely chiseled, shining with errands, motion and purpose.

My medical records in my arms, I squint at the blinding light and try to remember where I parked my car. I cross the road without noticing the traffic starting up, speedily, when the light turns green.

Safely on the other side, I gaze at the people laughing and talking excitedly into their phones, parking, meeting and greeting others. I watch them as if I were a character from a black and white movie who's ended up in a color film by mistake. Like a body-double who has lost the plot, acting without participating.

I find the car, turn on the engine and drive home.

I'm almost there, my destination already in sight, when a doubt, which had settled in some deep set recess until now, spreads through my mind: how am I going to manage? How can I carry on with everything as usual, feeling the way I'm feeling?

I park and get out but instead of heading home, I head for the woods.

Spring is glowing all around. The dead colors, darkness, cold and winter ice crusts have been torn off, pushed aside now by nature's forceful sap. The gaudy colors of the flowers and the frivolous undertones of the new leaves have also given way to this unblemished, solid green growth. Washed down by frequent strong rains, each plant is breathing and shining: it has made it through and overcome, winning another summer of life for itself.

These past weeks, ever since the cold alarm whiffs have been blowing at me, I have often come to this triumphant park. Hoping it could warm and nurture some hope; stir up some sap within me to carry me beyond the perils.

While walking along among the joggers, dog walkers and mums pushing their strollers (at supersonic speed, because being a mum doesn't mean giving up jogging), I let myself be swathed by this atmosphere, where people tend to their bodies and their time.

But the news I've been given, is slowly crystallizing into a frosty anxiety. The more I wander through the triumphant resurrection, the less I feel in sync with the season and people's routines.

Today, walking through the park only makes me feel like a useless outsider, dry brushwood, incapable of earning my way to spring.

I give up my stroll and take myself and my own small winter back home, knowing I'll have to be careful. I'll have to keep the cold worried whiffs in check and make sure I don't end up treacherously sneezing them all over the others.

"We were invited to Disney World, remember? They're waiting for an answer. How about it?" my husband asks, that night.

My fork is hanging in mid-air and everyone sitting around the dinner table is staring at me.

Disney World...

This trip belongs to a different script. A previous version which included possibilities, invitations, enthusiastic friends who go to Disney World every year and who, very kindly, offered to host us.

"Well... I don't know."

Disney World. Now?

Then again, there are previous engagements and the kids expectations... Plus the idea that maybe in Disney World my dearest kin will take less notice of me. And I'll finally be able to sneeze without everyone worrying about me.

Once in Disney World, among the palm trees and tropical lights, the silent film turns frantic. A real old time comedy, with actors jumping around full speed and glaring exaggerated smirks. On and off the little trains, into the 4D cinemas, melting in the sweaty and whiny queues that twist and turn around the kids wishes, for hours on end, under the—Oh so painfully hot!—Florida sun. The film rolls on then rewinds, repeating itself on each of the three days, with a few small variations: one day a cave full of happy-go-lucky characters, warriors from another galaxy on the next and sliding through water sprays the day after that.

My body double participates and submits, trampling on feet in the queues, shivering in the freezing caves of air conditioning that open up in every theater.

"Maybe... you shouldn't have come?" my friend wonders out loud.

"Actually it's good, really," I reassure her.

There's nothing to understand here, nothing to be part of. Everything is so abnormal and fake: six foot Mickey Mouse waving his hand, pirate ships, bogus forests and castles...

This is a place where desperation feels at ease.

You can grab onto the armrests, the popcorn, the heat and everyone's laughter, just like the kids grab onto the handlebars and swing along, one hand at a time. These moments of pre-packaged amusement carry me through to the end of the holiday. And I'm three days closer to the finale, whatever the outcome.

Like a tightrope walker

Some happy endings include dripping blood, sweat, grinding teeth and a letdown. After child birth, for instance, families celebrate the bundle of blessings rolled into that mishmash of genes and chromosomes the newborn is made of—meanwhile, the young mother lies in the corner of this collective joy, her eyes still damp. She has yet to get over the brutal strain and the feeling she's been betrayed by Nature. She's been clutched and gashed by pain for so long that, by the end, she's forgotten she should actually be in utter bliss.

I feel I've been through something similar when I hold the last medical report in my hands. The negative response telling me that all is well.

I've been through too many complications, operations gone wrong, fears and suffering. And now, as I put down the report I had awaited for so long, the only sound that manages to break out through the tangle of rage, weariness and letdowns which have smothered my disposition, is a sigh of relief.

I had decided to face the most delicate part of the matter in

Italy, with the kids. So, I'd flown across with my medical records full of unknown words, hoping I could find a way to undergo the operation there.

A dear friend came to pick us up in Fiumicino—the kids and I and all our luggage—and took us to her house in the country. It smelled of wood and freshly cut grass, of cleanliness and home. I slept off the hours of insomnia from the flight and the nights full of fears. Sleeping in her large, pristine bed I could feel something was beginning to flow the way it should; some connections, some small capillaries of energy were starting to function again.

Then, in Florence, I started finding words again, stereotypes and gestures which echoed within me, recalling things I knew, could understand and define. The looks on the doctors' faces, their attitudes, the bureaucratic rigmarole, the words in the diagnosis… Everything was suddenly so straightforward it seemed easy. I could finally judge the information about the disease, put things into perspective and look at them from every possible point of view.

With my loved ones and my friends around me, their smells, their voices, hugs and gestures, my flesh was back where it belonged, becoming connected and being nourished again.

I grew in strength and took my stand, fists in the air and feet firmly on the ground. I was ready to grab the illness by its horns, if I really was ill, and hurl it out of my life.

But then, as often happens, more alarms were added to the mix. An emergency suddenly landing on my plate full of troubles, throwing everything off balance.

"Why do I need the mask?"

"Don't worry Mum, it's just a precaution."

"Did you really have to call the ambulance?"

"Everything is going to be fine."

"Well, anyway, if I die, that's that."

"Come on, don't say that…"

"And no crying, ok?"

"Ok, no crying."

But where would your face be? That pale face behind the oxygen mask. The face all my feelings still rush to and curl up against seeking some warmth, milk, a smile.

No crying. But where would all my feelings go, Mum?

Days full of fear and confusion, fatigue, corridors, stretchers and small improvements followed.

Eventually my mother crawled out of danger and fought on, slowly getting better, barely standing. Frail and startled, but still with us.

"I've got a thick skin," she declared shakily.

Meanwhile her face cradled my deepest feelings.

But a shadow had surfaced among them. Because now the fear of losing her was upon me and threw its threatening shadow onto her ailing features.

Soon after, having found someone to take care of the kids, I went in for my operation. In the clinic where I was born, protected by something symbolic I couldn't pinpoint, I smiled, chatted with the doctors and nurses. I fell asleep full of trust.

I woke up feeling weird pains and my brother's hand wrapped around my hand.

My much older brother whom I hadn't shared a childhood with—the precious friend, always too far away—was by my side now, so close. His grasp so intimate, spreading a new soft warmth over my skin.

Then, suddenly, through the fuzziness of the morphine, a doctor appeared in my field of vision. My hazy eyes couldn't always keep him in focus, but I could still sense his awkwardness, the fact he was trying to find the right voice to deliver the bad news.

"There were some complications… We had to operate on you twice. Unfortunately what was supposed to be a routine check, became something more serious. There are some repercussions."

Bits that would need to be reconstructed with future operations. The external appearance would never be the same again.

I didn't even have the time to be saddened by the news because the morphine wasn't enough to stop the pulsing pain, bloated feeling and discomfort I had never felt before. Within a few hours, an internal hemorrhage had taken me back into the operating room for a third time.

For several weeks, while waiting for the outcome, I continued to feel weak from the blood I had lost, dizzy from all the anesthetics and shocked by my body and my life's sheer vulnerability.

So now that it's all over, now that the medical reports tell me I had nothing to fear, now that I could start standing straight and bold again, I'm still slouching around, wobbly, sliding slowly along like a tight-rope walker. Wavering on the thin line between health and safety. Suspended over an abyss of dangers and unexpected events.

"Everything's ok, right, Mum? Why are you still worried?"
"Yes, everything's fine. I'm not worried."
Except I can't seem to get rid of the way I'm feeling and the way I'm walking, slowly sliding along.
"Mum, do you want to go for a walk?"
We take a walk through the wild hills bathed in a warm sunset.

They are agile, looking around, swiftly running around and improvising "last one there is an idiot" races. I advance one step at a time, the fatigue of the operation weighing on every fiber in my body.

I look at my hands, which are too pale, and think about this wary way of life that is sticking to me like an infected fungus. But, somehow, I don't even want to shake it off.

"Mum, look, a firefly!"
Precious fireflies. Suspended in mid air, blinking a verse, here and there, in these long summer evenings. "There is a meaning, somewhere. A spark of joy that surfaces, lights up every now and then, can you see it? It's here… no, over here… and here… and here…"

There are only a few this evening. Flying shyly, far from one another, as the twilight slowly puts out the colors of the bushes and wild shrubs.

"Mum, we're going back to the States soon, and then what?"
Right, then what? I find it hard to take a stand while feeling this way. Finding a path to my liking, contemplating an activity—it all seems impossible.

I stroll along and remember hiking up these paths and in these woods when I was a little girl.

"I loved going up the creeks. I would get lost sometimes, scratch myself and tear my trousers. But I never stopped."

"Really? You never got scared?"

"No, I never got scared."

Walking was like being in a safe dimension, a nowhere land. I was completely free, unreachable, far from everyone and everything, far from danger.

"Even in the city?"

"I always liked wandering around, without a destination. Just wandering off with no money or ID papers."

"Why?"

"Because I didn't want to have to carry anything, I wanted to feel light. I would walk for hours. Down streets, along the river, through the suburbs…"

"Why did you walk so much?"

"Who knows…"

Maybe because I preferred exploring the world instead of living in it…

"And when you grew up?"

"I walked even further! With minimum luggage, just the few things I could fit in a backpack."

All my past, all my needs would be in it. And on I went, on and on.

Through the continuous moment, the never ending instant… Being suspended while everything is flowing by. Beyond everything but also in the midst of it all; traveling through the world and feeling at the centre of it. Without missing a thing, without hiding or running away. No getting involved or depending. No getting tied up, doing or starting anything. No giving up, making mistakes or encounters, no misinterpreting. In the face of it all, just going on and on. With all your might. Without missing a thing.

"Kids, I have a plan. When we get back to the States, we'll take a trip!"

Making it through

The minimum luggage is now made up of enormous bags and suitcases and the means of transport are a plane and finally a large car. But what really matters is that each one of us is all there, without dragging along a trail of obligations, without drooling on frustrations or expectations. We each have everything we need and which identifies us in a suitcase.

The landscape seems suspended beyond something. The sky-scape starts out blue and infinite, spreading out high above, beyond the small portholes of the airplane.

Then comes the urban landscape, beyond the car windows, with streets floating above the heat mirage. Low, square built houses, sometimes grey, other times colored. Cube-shaped television studios. Billboards. Electricity poles with long, dangling wires.

The wires don't weave through trees and vines like in Maryland because there are very few plants here. Just a few rows of palm trees along the main avenues and, here and there, some agave and small succulents.

We're in the south, the desert is nearby and there's no shade; the strong California sunshine oversees everything. Light dazzling the soft rumps of the Los Angeles hills.

Anyway it would all be the same to me right now; even if there were scenes from another world or I were at a different latitude. Here or anywhere else, I would still feel this denial, filled with wellbeing, flowing through me as do the scenes out there... A murky, generous feeling that stays with me even when we stop and step out of the car.

Like when the landscape turns into very long avenues, and a golden star bearing the name of a celebrity is set in every step of the pavement.

The girls walk along silently looking around.

"It's like being in a movie..." declares the eldest, her sweet chestnut gaze lost in a daydream.

"Yeah, but not just one film in particular," I add. "It feels like being inside all of them, in the very essence of movies."

As if the thousands of movies produced in the area had saturated the air, the sidewalks and buildings; and in some way, by simply strolling down the street, we were part of it all, making them and watching them all at the same time.

I almost regret lowering my head and deflecting my mind from this illusion but, at some point, the temptation becomes too strong. I can't resist the appeal of reading out loud this sort of roll-call: the names of past glories engraved in the golden stars. Jazz singers, actors from silent movies, celebrities from the "white telephone" films, bluesmen, showmen… They're all there, at our feet.

My eyes meanwhile jump ahead to the next star, and the one after that ("Who's that over there?"), until I get caught up in a sort of frenzy and I have to look at them all.

"Look, I've found Bill Evans! Over here, there's Chuck Berry! Hey, look: Groucho Marx!" I call out through the people walking by. Eventually I realize I'm the only one becoming so excited.

The second daughter smiles, her blue, understanding eyes silently telling me she gets it, loves me and is trying to be thrilled by the same things that thrill me, but these names mean nothing to her.

To her as to millions of other people… Hordes of emotionless tourists stepping over them every day, their eyes scouring for the latest celebrity. And to me too; as I slide past so many stars whose names don't spark any memories in my brain!

The Hollywood Boulevard film suddenly stops.

The pizza parlors, cinemas, theaters, shops selling wigs and families licking ice creams, girls faking shrieks of excitement, kids hanging out of strollers, the fanatics setting up tripods to take shots of the stars on the sidewalks… This enormous, glorified monument to everything ephemeral grinds to a halt and becomes quiet.

Somewhere offscreen a voice is whispering. The voice of past films, celebrities and engraved names. The dead, forgotten sound of unknown lives, unmade-up faces, old fashions.

"All the world's a stage, and all the men and women merely players," wrote the great poet who staged all our human troubles. But here, on Hollywood Boulevard, it seems more like a large dressing room full of human smells, slippers and tired bodies. A dressing room welcoming us, checking out our make-up and the faces we pull. It allows us to play different roles. Print out names and engrave handprints, get excited and shine. It welcomes us and smiles, until the next actor comes along. It has seen so many already and there are so many more to come…

"What's happening, Mum? Dad, what are these guys waiting for?"

Beyond the stars and thoughts, we have reached the Chinese Theater. The one with the pagoda-shaped entrance and a small forecourt where celebrities leave their handprints in the concrete.

A crowd has assembled.

"They are waiting for some famous actor to turn up. For a film premiere, I suppose."

"Can we wait too? Come on, let's wait!"

We squeeze into the twitching crowd, waiting to look through heads and shoulders to catch a glimpse of an actor getting out of a car, waving to the fans and walking into the theater.

Meanwhile, all these passionate spectators nonchalantly trample all over the large and small handprints set in the concrete by past celebrities.

To undying memory.

I don't feel like staying here, being pushed around and rubbing shoulders and legs. I've never understood how people could wait for hours on end to then yell out and wave to a celebrity. I feel embarrassed, like when I see someone crying his eyes out in the street or watch two people hurling insults at one another. Sloppy, over-the-top feelings, that are even a bit contrived.

The most I can offer to our little committee is to continue hunting down names. We bend over again and root around, sweeping the concrete blocks with our eyes.

"Here it is, I found it!!! Look, Harrison Ford's star!"

The middle daughter has finally found the name the old and young fans can all agree upon.

And we also all agree to join the Universal Studios tour. How can we possibly resist? In Los Angeles, films become part of your breathing, dreams and decisions. You can't get away: the witchcraft of the entertainment industry manipulates our imagination. It has raised us ever since we were toddlers after all. Shaping our heroes and reactions before we even got to know them. So it's reassuring and right—almost necessary—to go and have a look at the place where it all began.

And, surprise: the tour becomes a journey within a journey.

Riding the little train that takes us through the Studios, everything flows, no stopping, no holding back. The flow almost becomes liquid as the little train travels up and down the soft hills scattered with film sets.

We cross fake roads and fake squares, villages, rivers and bits of bays.

"I recognize this road!"

"This one too, but... I thought it was in New York!"

We've seen them in lots of films, as if various stories were set on the same street corner. Instead, the same cardboard street was being used in different productions. We would recognize them and feel these bits of a non-existent world belonged to us. Or maybe we just knew they didn't really exist. In our hearts a warning would go off, pointing out that something wasn't quite right, but we silenced it: "Leave me alone, I'm watching a film!" Who cares if it's using the same tricks as hundreds of others, I have paid my brain a ticket, taken a seat in the dimmed story and complied. Now show me something, take me somewhere!

The little train meanwhile takes us through a bit of collapsed subway, past the Psycho motel, along the flowered streets of Wisteria Lane...

The train too tells us shreds of stories.

Just like a movie or a tale, it carries us through the emotions of an atmosphere and allows us to breath in a scene. Then away we go again, on to something else, up and down the soft hills.

This train is a perfect metaphor. Describing so well our imagination's journey, our path through words and wonders, through the images and trepidation of a story...

We enter a 4D tunnel: a dark jungle. We penetrate a lush vegetation amidst sounds of tropical animals.

Suddenly the train stops.

We jump in fear to the sound of gigantic steps and mysterious roars. What's happening? Turning towards the tail end of the train we see a tyrannosaurus has grabbed the last carriage in its claws! It shakes it, tears it away from the other carriages and throws it to the side. Then turns towards us and drops of saliva drip onto our faces (for real!). We are its next target!

More roars emerge from the heart of the forest, new steps thudding, coming close, echoing in our stomachs. The plants open wide and reveal a new beast: Godzilla. He's engaging the tyrannosaurus in a fierce battle to save us, hurray! Thuds, roars and blows fly through the air while the little train takes off again and we are saved.

Outside the tunnel, in the sunlight and away from the dinosaurs, we take a few minutes to catch our breath and chuckle.
"I thought I was having a heart attack."
"Can we do it again?"
Sure we can. It was so thrilling.
But… we hadn't actually done anything. We hadn't moved a muscle in our brain. We'd let ourselves be frightened, excited and moved in a continuous, easy flow of emotions. It was all so real! Right there in front of us, at the fingertips of all our senses.
No leaps, no obstacles. No long, hard or even quick and easy journey through a book, a screening or a concert or whatever. No discovery, no spell. Just total, instant enjoyment: it's so handy. Like being transported on a conveyor belt instead of walking.
Will this kind of entertainment really catch on? Will this imagination conveyor become the future of entertainment?
Meanwhile, we course along happily—on the Studios train and the conveyor belt—and reach another tunnel that takes us through an Egyptian pyramid to the centre of the Earth.

We come out with happy legs and unsteady minds, which have been opened to wonders and haven't quite shut. We expect a gust of surprises, from some corner of the Studios, to suddenly blow into the wind of our emotions and lift them here and there, light and unpredictable again.
And that's exactly what happens, again and again.
And again with the stuntmen's show—we can't not be amazed. Those men and those women have turned their bodies into immortal tools. What plane do they live on? How do they use our same dimensions when they throw themselves in the air, fall, get kicked and run through fire. Watching them fly over objects and through space like no one else could possibly even imagine doing, I wonder how many planes the real world is actually made of.

It can't just be a matter of training. It can't only be about hard work, sweat, strong muscles and agility. It's more about feeling and moving freely through the air, viewing space and your body through a lens of risks and skills, where everything is allowed and nothing causes pain.

"No chance of getting hurt, and even less of dying…"[4] someone used to sing about the guy walking barefoot on shards of glass.

It's what happens with the jugglers, acrobats, tamers, trapeze and circus artists and body doubles in action movies… all living in that different dimension where they never get hurt and never die. At least, almost never.

I think about myself, my dimension: hard-edged, rough, unstable and a bit slimy. My cautious movements, always fearing the worst.

The audience pours out while the artists are still taking their bows and somersault off the stage. We remain in our seats watching the flips fade away.

Then, finally, after so many months, I feel like crying.

California I'm coming home

Vast, dry and luminous spaces open wide from one side to the other of the horizon, on the California coast. We drive down the middle of it all as the landscapes, beyond the windows, blow by non-stop, faster than the wind.

The images slide by all around us and we comment, choose and decide.

"No, I don't feel like stopping here; let's go on."

So on we go, with the radio blaring.

Just like the landscapes rolling past our eyes, the music rolls down the open lands of our minds as they peacefully scan, comment, choose or rest.

We all play the game: we look out the windows, make cheerful comments, and when we come across something beautiful worth pointing out or grabbing hold of, we call out: "Here, here, can we stop here?"

Other times, we get carried away by the sway of the engine,

the electronic games or a guide book, and put our thoughts into neutral.

We also allow ourselves to be surprised.

From the information in the guide book, Santa Barbara had brought to mind a small sea town, like the ones in Italy; the holiday town of a nearby big city. A sea resort with easy going people dressed in pale colors, a stroll through roads with a somewhat Mexican feel: white and a bit squared off. Crowds on the beach, marinas filled with boats and evening strolls down the main streets.

In reality, Santa Barbara is more like the weird funny reflection of a deforming mirror. Because it turns out to be precisely the way our minds' pixels had shaped it out to be—with the same colors, layout and atmospheres—but everything is enlarged, dislodged here and there, with only a handful of people and rarefied sounds.

Even after so many months in the States, the luxury of space they have here still surprises me. The fact they can build houses that don't come anywhere near one another, even viewed in perspective; roads that stretch out through vast meadows and beaches that make your sight strain to an unreachable point.

Marinas with large boats, in wide berths, along peaceful jetties. The wind apparently adapted to the style, barreling, unstoppable, through the broad openings, lifting specks, bending ropes and shaking hawsers.

The sea is boundless, smiling and calm when we get there. The deep blue waves swarm to the coastline, one after the other, spattered with bright seagull spots.

At first glance, it looks just like our sea in Italy. Gazing into the distance, it too bursts out into an unbroken vista. In the Mediterranean, you know it will end somewhere, against an invisible obstacle that's not too far away, whereas here (maybe due to the different light, a different shade of color or perhaps a geographic awareness) looking out over the horizon, you sense a different sort of vastness and unknown.

Whereas the sand dunes of the county park, a few miles further north, are definitely larger than those in the Mediterranean.

They are as vast as a horizon, with only a few lagoons cradled between them. They banish every other land formation, vegetation and possible man-made construction from sight. A white, wooden boardwalk extending down to the sea is the only reminder of mankind, of human endeavor, of motion.

Everything is still and silent.

Teeming with lagoon life; intense activity on the water surface bubbling with eggs, low flying birds, a gentle breeze through the reeds and yellow reflections. In total silence, flattened down to earth by the low, white sky covering the dunes like the door of a coffer. Nothing can escape, nothing can change in this motionless universe, silently waiting, since the beginning of time.

We are among a handful of visitors: a few Mexican families, with plenty of little radios and beach chairs, bags and mats, stepping along the boardwalk ten meters behind us. They too are unusually silent. Going down to the seashore, to the beach, dressed the way we would be in Italy: towels around their necks, sand buckets, flip flops and T-shirts. I watch them and shiver under my layers of sweaters, fleece and a pile jacket. A stiff, damp, cold wind is blowing and the Mexican families resemble aliens who have landed on the wrong shore by mistake.

"Mothership, have you made a mistake? It's freezing cold here!"

"Affirmative, advance team, there's been a mixup. But the mission is confirmed. I repeat the mission is confirmed: just pretend all is well and proceed!"

When we reach the beach, I watch them get installed: they set the tables, chairs and radios and suddenly blare out. The grown-ups laugh and play jokes, the little ones shriek as they jump into the icy looking, and undoubtedly icy cold, water.

Where have they hidden their spaceship?

We too get installed, stiff in the holes we have dug against the wind, and watch the pelicans and seagulls gliding through the low streams of wind.

From my hole, I see everything flowing by. The images of dunes and birds, my son forging canals and constructions with small bits of wood which have been washed ashore, the movements of the Mexican families defying the wind and the cold, eating around a camping table. Everything is just flowing by.

Crouched in the sand hole out of the wind, surrounded by fragments of wood, seagulls and picnic tables, I feel, for an instant, that there are no more roads to go down, neither on the rope nor off it. It's just a matter of gently landing on the ground.

If only it could last forever...

I could just walk away from the journey, with no regrets.

Allowing myself to just stop and connect.

Without focusing on the future or being entangled in past nets.

Just living, moving along from one perspective to the next, from one encounter to the next. Fear: a slight, passing, annoyance, like a sneeze, that suddenly crops up and is just as suddenly forgotten...

Like water trickling down the grooves traced by a child's finger in the sand: when a grain moves or a twig is set across the flow, thoughts discover a new bed and spill into it on their own.

So, now that we are on Highway 1, jolting along the Big Sur landscapes, I feel my mind flowing somewhere else, in an unknown direction.

The park is snuggled in between the mountains and the ocean. A single tongue of road running through it, all ups and downs. At one point it's suspended over a cliff—rocks capped with indomitable woods on one side and rocks diving into inaccessible coves on the other. Then, after a steep down slope, it leans on a flat land with pastures and cows grazing here and there. Then up another incline, with impenetrable rocks and a waterfall hurling water down to the beach.

With hot stretches in the sun: roll down the windows ("Give me my sunglasses"), eyes rejoicing in the bright landscapes. Followed by dark, cold planes covered in fog: bring on the prescription glasses ("Close them now, aren't you cold?"). All around a faint, spooky light, barely unveiling the road.

Our car swerves, alone, along the uphill slopes and hairpin descents, engulfed by smells full of nature; damp dribbles blurring the sunset. And I watch, inhale and drive, while a forgotten sensation trickles back into my mind. A slight pulsing sense of belonging; the right to be alive, every single moment.

These places have been the destination of many people's journeys: minstrels, writers, wayfarers. They have all come through here, been carried along, gotten lost. All touched by these lights and these whiffs of sea. "Each one along his journey, and each one so different,"[5] as the guy in the Roxy Bar used to sing.

These corners of the world's steep coastlines have been crowded with travelers for decades. Many a page, many a note, have detailed those journeys. Like sparkling reflections of cut diamonds sent out to shine around the world. Bits of journeys stretching out over the continents.

"These landscapes were in so many of my teenage dreams..."

As well as the journeys through them, the songs and words painting countless different images coming to me from so far away.

Taking off. Getting lost. Finding oneself again.

Just feeling what you feel. Without any knowledge of before or after. Just being yourself, your own hands tucked into the pockets of your destiny. Being enough to serve your own purpose, which is to have no purpose at all. Loose hair, soiled with life. The intense essence of the unknown and change burning your skin.

So many winds have blown over those faces. So many jackets have been flung along the fancy-free routes of motorbikes bending down these hairpin turns...

And now *I* too am here, on these cliffs.

I've stepped out of the car. Looking at the sea, with my short hair and clean face. My arms tightly gripping a windbreaker to protect myself from all bad weather and all unexpected events.

This should be the right place, after all.

My mind leaping as it should, like a goat running up and down the cliffs, grazing tasty fantasies. I let it romp around freely.

We walk down to a wind-beaten cove with rocks chafed by the tides into nooks and caves, single-standing rocks and an archway out at sea for us to admire from the shore.

We are all bundled up in our windbreakers, pinning down

our sweaters, scarves tied around our sun hats and hoodies. We are quite a show, but undoubtedly less majestic than the natural surroundings.

I try taking a picture of the stone arch, the wind throwing me off balance and the sand and salt whirling around, sneaking into the invisible nooks and crannies of our clothes, lips and eyelashes. My fingers are desperately trying to protect the camera, but they can't, and it breaks.

I stand still, soaking in the unique seascape: the sun, in agreement with the rocks, is setting right behind them in a triumph of sorrowful, yellow rays; the strength of the waves receding with the light.

How I wish I could freeze this moment.
Like all the others I've taken pictures of in my life.
Excursions and encounters, landscapes, first steps, a road…
I wish I could put off oblivion, keep a speck of past moments, and eventually revive them again later, repeating the replay option, indefinitely.

And not just with photographs. The old postcards, birthday cards, outgrown baby clothes and toys they sucked on when they were in their cots… Each object is magical; within it all the beauty, smells, tastes and precise vibration of that moment. I must keep it, guard it jealously from the inescapable passing of time and memory's continuous grinding of recollections to make room for new impressions. I'm always duped into believing I will, sooner or later, be able to reclaim an era, bring it back to life thanks to small snippets of memory and a few left over objects.

In a sort of familial Jurassic Park, the bygone curd-stained playsuit should recreate my baby's sweet, milky smell and the warmth of the room, the sound of the music box and gurgles hovering in the air, the pale colored paint on the walls, the tight air creating the unique and sacred space full of light I used to roam holding my newborn child…

What's all this got to do with Kerouac and the Big Sur, with empty, wild, hippie freedom, the trips, rebellion and not giving a fuck about anything, which my imagination has celebrated for so long?

I crave the big wide world but all I seem to hold on to are shreds of dead eras.

If not now, on the west coast of the States. So far away, so lost, but at the heart of dreams… If not now, when?
Why not open the doors of my trappings?
Pour out all the thousands of photographs, books, old comics, play dough figurines, friends' gifts… And away, in the saddle of a motorbike, letting them take flight behind me, by the handful, as I watch them float away.

The sun is resting in the sea, now. Rays, crowning it from above, plunge in and spill over the water in blinding shafts. Their shining bits of light, disrupted by the waves, reach the shore. Their self-moving glow is like a phrase repeating itself, the message nature exhales at all times, which finally seeps into my mind: time is but time, it passes.

It doesn't exist on its own. We can't live it, ride it, grab on to slow it down or push to make it accelerate. Or even recreate it with magic objects.
Each particle moving in the universe, migrating from one state to another, each fractional, unstoppable shift in the evolution of matter, carries objects and people from one time to another of their existence.
And here I stand, thinking I could actually thwart the process!
Open the doors and let it all out: the broken objects or those that have disappeared; the people who have died and all past experiences.
Feeling giddy, a vision of levity makes me embrace the idea of an existence keyed on total abandonment, on the true, unshakeable, trusting knowledge that everything happens as it should.

I put away the camera, tighten my jacket around the gaps full of wind. I look at the sun which has almost disappeared into the distant reddish mist above the ocean. Then, call out "Let's go!" over the laughter of the children chasing one another on the beach. I too laugh, within: what a fool I've been, thinking I could jam the motion of the Universe with my basement full of junk.

The time game

Particles shift, imperceptibly.

Thoughts trickle down the canal I've drawn, without realizing, next to the bits of wood my son used, and ideas flow down a new path. Circling the journey and lifting it, bending it and shifting it onto a different axis.

It's no longer a matter of gliding through. My safe mind and strong keel emit waves of awareness, irritation and admiration that spearhead places and explore situations.

The sand of Carmel's long beach is cold and damp. The mist clears only by short intervals, the sea is barely visible before disappearing. The houses beyond the beach also come in and out of white drizzles of fog. Remembering it later on, it feels like it could have been a dream. The farthest of lands possible.

Yet, it's precisely here that, in an unexpected flicker, my mind finally sheds an opinion again.

Strung alongside one another, the houses are all different, alternating slight variations in style: a bit more lodge, a bit more Mediterranean, a bit more Old England, a bit more Far West... Still, everything is sober and elegant, with large windows showing interiors rich in creativity, comfort, joy in being in a good place and being there with a very personal, wise sense of identity.

We are with the same friends from last year, those we had shared the corners of Maine with. And I find myself in a similar situation: they are enthralled by so much privileged elegance whereas I glare out through the heavy, damp mist that weighs down on everything, almost erasing the sea and the beach from view. A beautiful beach, no doubt, stretching to infinity. But it's hardly visible.

Yet again, all this graceful prosperity, these perfect structures set in one of the most expensive corners of the United States where we, the educated, rich and refined, are always wanting to be together... Why is it they only ever want to be among their peers? Wanting to spend their holidays in a place with such horrible weather all year round just to be part of this community, to belong?

"What is it? What's bothering you?"

"It's too much…"

From the free, windy cliffs travelers of all times continue journeying along, urged on by the inability to feel content with the established order of things, down to this beach where those who so love the niche they're in, they actually dug a hole and are up to their necks in it…

"The gap is too wide."

We leave the beach, sinking our feet in the sand squeaking damp wealth.

Meanwhile I wonder: can a wretched earthling not choose a different route? Can one not live a more balanced existence, where freedom and choices, play and stop, are in tune?

The answer I get, soon after, is supplied by a peculiar guy, the sort of person one often comes across in the United States. Here, more than in any country I have visited, there are people who roam the world with the same airiness stuntmen have when they somersault through different dimensions.

Wherever they go, these people always feel they belong, and rightly so. For them, it's not a matter of feeling alive and connected to only a few specific places. The world is their plaything: a fascinating, dangerous place to journey through, at their own ease and comfort, seeking new paths and more suitable lifestyles.

"Jump on guys, jump on. And you, little one, can take the helm as soon as we are out at sea!"

The fisherman, our host onboard, left Sicily when he was a teenager. He's short, tanned and strong, his skin carved by the sun and the wind like all fishermen at the four corners of the Earth.

He's calm and confident. We, instead, are less at ease, my youngest steering the fishing boat through the enormous bay of Monterey while we hang on as best we can to every hold we find and try to ignore the ocean's long swells.

Meanwhile, the fisherman tells us about this ocean's routines. The calm sea in the bay giving way to high waves and strong winds as soon as you stick your bow out beyond the head, the chill freezing every breath and your hands becoming frostbitten from working in the cold. And when he recalls what it was like fishing in Sicily, his smile opens wide and his wrinkles softly move to the corners of his face. His eyes narrow with each memory.

"Yeah… the sun was always so strong, it was always so hot, even at dawn we'd be out fishing in T-shirts, singing and whistling. It ain't like that here. Here it's all chattering teeth and I just want to go home!"

But he didn't think twice about leaving the warm sea where he used to sing as a boy. He jumped onto one of those cosmic shifts that drag some people from one side of the planet to the other. It hasn't got anything to do with tickets and ferries, planes or ships. It's all about hardcore energy and movements guided by strong will, opportunities and slipping into invisible currents.

So the fisherman worked hard and bought himself a boat here, in California, and one in Alaska where he goes salmon fishing once a year.

"One trip to Alaska and I'm set for the rest of the year. I fish here in Monterey too, but with no stress. With two months in Alaska, I put away enough money to not have to worry."

He can allow himself to take it easy and spend a whole month doing repairs. Peacefully cleaning his boat, stripping, sanding and painting it. He shows it off proudly. It was a war vessel, used in Vietnam. With a good keel, lots of space and leakproof. So he had the weapons removed and loaded it with nets. He's been sailing it for years.

And he can allow himself to be a lazybones for one afternoon, with these Italians on holiday—who he happened to meet in a car park—and tell them his life stories, show them the bay and the wildlife.

The sea lions—gigantic, dark, cylindrical lumps—are stretched out on vast rocky wharfs that protect the beaches of Monterey from the vigor of the open sea. Piled on top of one another, their flippers wide open and necks turned upwards. They growl long throaty sounds and reek of shit to high heaven. Their pups pop out from the heap of snouts, necks, bellies and flippers and look a bit lost even though they are in the safest spot they could ever be.

My little one, meanwhile, is steering the fishing boat, alert and proud. The fisherman is supervising and smiling, or maybe just tightening his eyes against the glaring sunshine, I can't really tell. His voice is mellow as he explains, points out and gazes at the sea. Delicately slowing the engine down, he pilots the large hull right up to the otters. Small, long and thin, they sleep with enormously long algae tentacles wrapped around their bodies.

"Otherwise the sea would sweep them away."

Luckily these algae grow forty meters up from the bottom of the sea to cuddle the soft, thick coats of these little creatures. It's flipping me out seeing them so still in the freezing water. But obviously they don't feel the cold, with the blubber, fur and stuff they secrete just to be able to lay there, wrapped in spirals of algae with very long, jagged tentacles. Their gentle otter eyes are closed as they all hug a little one. Almost all. They hold their cub tight because the algae aren't enough to stop the strong ocean tides from dragging it away.

We say goodbye to the fisherman in the windy bay and, soon after, on a hairpin turn of Route 1, we say goodbye to our friends. They had come from the north and are continuing south, mirroring our journey. We hooked up briefly half way along, and now go our separate ways.

I watch them walk towards their car and fleetingly get a sense of the meters, tens, hundreds and thousands of kilometers they have just started putting between us with those first few steps. I see them going back to that faraway place where our other friends, acquaintances and families live. I see them reconnecting with what we have left behind. Then, they turn around one last time: "We'll call you from Florence!" and wave goodbye.

I get back in the car, slip on my sunglasses for the handful of curves along the coast that are still basking in the sun and start singing an old hit. The Canadian singer travelled the world, the song goes, but when she came to California she felt at home.

Towards the end

As we move inland, the landscape becomes more and more sun-drenched and barren. We glide up and down soft hills and their never-ending slopes, covered in never-ending vineyards, almond orchards, cut maize and empty fields where big, slow cows graze on yellow grass. There's nothing intensive in this part of the world, let alone animal farming. No wonder the milk is tasty, the butter is tasty, and so is the fruit sold piecemeal to those driving by, from wooden huts standing next to large warehouses.

All the towns seem to be full of dust and hardship. The dingy houses, patched up with anything available, are equipped with bare essentials. Several, actually almost all of them, are large prefabricated, one-piece boxes. With just one floor, a metal fence around it and a wonky swing hanging from a branch. And the American flag, nearby, fluttering from a tall, white pole.

We happen to see one traveling along the road, wide and slow.

"Hey, look, that tractor is pulling a house! Don't they build houses normally here, Mum?"

"Well… not always; they build these somewhere else then park them on a small piece of land."

Some of these big boxes are churches and have small, badly mowed and badly watered lawns out front. And neon signs promising prayers, songs and the love of God. Everything openly displayed, with the service hours listed on the roadside, as if it were a local theater house.

Other prefabs are restaurants, with asphalt parking lots and neon signs that join names of people to names of dishes (Tom's Steak, Gigi's Pizza, Old Ma's Pie) and grimy smells all around.

Placed one above the other, these houses could resemble the small flats in any European apartment building, any average block of flats, and the people living there could cut down on utilities, spend less and live more comfortably.

But then again, I realize they wouldn't be able to. Americans, even the poorest, have to distance themselves from others. Have their own things, their moving space, their independence, far from eyeshot and earshot of others. It may be just a hut, but it must have space around it. If it's yours, you've got to have free rein.

I've never minded living in a block of flats. It has always reassured me, made me feel at home. Like having a big family above, below and all around me, with people who share my same rituals: in and out for school, work, illnesses, mourning...

A family with different personalities: agreeable or ill-tempered, invisible, discreet, loud and so on.

I used to like hearing someone's television set, in my nights of mental solitude. Or, during hot afternoons with open windows, hearing the children upstairs playing the piano. I liked feeling somehow inside a creature breathing, suffering or happily welcoming the good weather, the seasons and other everyday matters.

I'd also loved living in the country. The heroic, open spaces, the strong connection with what nourishes and what kills. Pears and vipers, crevasses and green fields. I'd even lived there alone, over some stretches of time, the isolation allowing me to observe every sound at night, every change of light during the day. So much time and concentration all around. Days pulsing a primeval breath, oozing scents and purity. Bathed in a crystal clear strength that could purify everything, even fear and solitude.

And there were no emissions around me. None of the millions of waves which, in the city, spill out of aerials, transmitting devices, medical equipment and telephones. And no ads, no traffic signs, no voices calling out or status symbols.

In the absence of electromagnetic fields and the presence of semantic clarity, my spirit was freer and lighter, and could even enjoy the isolation.

Whereas in the city, our soul is always cluttered with sounds and signs, everyone's claims to this or that, expectations, information... How can we not wish to seek out our peers? Try raising together a phalanx against the chagrins of life? Not want to reecho our own joyful moments with other people?

Space, again. Always in first place, the origin of everything.

For centuries, people have come to the States to flee danger or free themselves from others, the impositions of some culture or religion, or poverty. Whereas in Italy, ever since the beginning of time, we do the best we can with what we've got because what can't be cured must be endured.

So, we make a virtue of all the crowds of people and thoughts, and live tightly crammed together, trying to put up with one another, quarreling as little as we can (although it doesn't always work). We Italians are long and narrow, we can't get that far away from one another: inevitably piled on top of each another, fighting, making friends, getting along and elbowing our way through — that's how we live.

But there's more to it. With so little space, some places are inevitably intended for the community: squares, riverfronts, public gardens… Italian cities have a great number of places where people can meet, without having to spend money or belong to a certain social class. In the States instead, there are very few of these places. Some cities don't have any at all. So it's up to each individual to create a space he can live in, beyond the four walls of his home. Where he can express himself, feel welcome and protected. Where he is allowed.

The matter of space is not so trivial. Here, along the sunny Californian roads, I realize how important it is for a community to have a collective project: design places for itself where children can play, youngsters meet up and old people take walks. The only alternative is to carve out your own private corner. With your own means. Wherever you can.

In California's inlands, the box houses with burnt yards are strung out at a fair distance from one another. As soon as a small town comes to an end, the homes spread and thin out, leaving room for empty spaces, dotted with isolated items.

A store, a filling station, a farm.

And junk.

The remains of a pick up truck in a backyard.

A store with shattered windows in the middle of nowhere.

A typical Far West windmill with small blades hovering above a squat wooden tower.

A gas station gnawed by the wind.

We can't resist and have to get out to observe them as if these residues of who knows what were crucial monuments.

"I feel like I'm in a movie…"

My husband says it this time, the wind carrying his words and ruffling his hair. And I can imagine the movie. A movie with great expanses and stranded objects, a movie like a thousand others telling terrible, heroic stories. The images spelling out the hardships of living here, with no chorus commenting, no elbowing with other people's emotions.

The windmill blades creak in the silence and make you feel strong and exclusive like the hero of an on-the-road movie because you are alone, the only person there watching them turn. The cars driving by on the nearby road are deadpan.

We get back in the car but I want us to feel even freer and more lost. I dream of walking in the wind, galloping down a barren hill on horseback or ending the day under the stars.

But buildings start reappearing and the spell is over. Here and there, at a distance, we spot gigantic square farmhouses, built with wooden beams and wide sloping roofs. They're just like the ones in Maryland. But here, in California, they have chipped paint, rickety fences and dusty, bumpy white roads leading up to them.

We are tired and hungry. Rather than riding out into the night, now I just want some food and a bed. I'm dreaming of a shower and laying down without putting any more kilometers under my belt.

Instead, we continue running up our mileage along roads with more and more dusty, blinding, tiny towns full of motels and hotels that are already full. And miserable houses and farmhouses which haven't considered renting a room to foreigners in a million years.

I ponder the difference between the average European, bent on making a deal, and the empyreal, superior resignation of agricultural America, surrendering to its fate. America, Land of Opportunity. Here too?

We are approaching the national attraction, the great Yosemite park, and all the great American tourism chains have sold out. We read all the usual names which identify accommodations according to their styles. All the cheap motels, decent motels and luxury motels, have no vacancies. We drive in behind two other cars with fathers getting out, rushing into the reception and coming out shaking their heads, dejected. There's no hope. After all, the neon sign on the road had already made it clear that there were no rooms available, but exhaustion causes senseless actions and our own pater familias also gets out and skips along to the reception, chirps a few unhopeful sentences and comes out shaking his head.

We Mediterraneans are used to quick and easy deals and everyday horse trading for a good bargain, cash in hand. There's no need for big entrepreneurs or big capital: if I have something you need, you can have it and pay me for it.

We, the parents, have slept on roofs in Greece, corridors in Spain, a garage in Turkey, as well as eaten in a beduin's tent in Syria and under a fisherman's awning in Lebanon.

But everything here is better organized: it's a matter of strategy and big figures, planning and high level management.

Small independent stores are rare. All commercial businesses are run by big chains you can find all over the States. From sewing goods to drugs, hairdressers to gyms, office supplies, furniture, books, everything is very large scale, with enormous, standardized business plans. You can find the same products, in the same colors, the same shop windows and the same prices at every latitude and in every type of landscape. Thousands and thousands of businesses, all exactly the same.

Nothing is left to chance and very little to small enterprises. They set things up, study the field and pay for permits. But are all their market studies really that effective? We and thousands of other tourists can't find a place to sleep anywhere near Yosemite. Someone must have done the maths wrong.

I feel like arguing with them, now that I'm so tired and hungry. I'd really like to slap the wrist of those know-it-all marketing directors who planned so few rooms. So, I too get out of the car this time, with my husband. And now we both come back with our heads down.

Luckily, after chirping left and right, we track down a small apartment.

"We don't normally offer it because it's not great and needs some repairs."

I'm glad to see that my husband and I, with one voice, both declare: "It doesn't matter, really, it'll be fine for us!"

Sleeping in the most uncomfortable nooks and crannies the Mediterranean has to offer has its benefits: when it comes to adapting, we are among the best.

With the kids in tow, we rush into the little apartment in need of repairs, cheeringly explode our suitcases and turn the place into our pen for the next four days.

Sliding away

The apartment in bad shape isn't even too far away: we have about an hour's drive, each day, to get to the park. Which equates to nothing much in this part of the world.

A beautiful ramble through the valley gets us to the hut where we pay our entrance fee to the smiling, grey-green ranger leaning out of his little window. And we are suddenly in a new, vast, wild dimension.

A world opening onto curves, stretching behind gorges, below tall peaks and above deep canyons, with unlimited perspectives.

The scenery meanders up and down mountains brutalized by prehistoric disasters. Lava and earthquakes, fault lines, gashes and erosion… A violent hand has thrown bits here and there, like an impetuous, mad painter wanting at all cost to amaze viewers with dramatic combinations. And he has succeeded.

The rocky mountain peaks were pushed apart by titanic forces which raised them and dug them up, joined their peaks with lava fires, blended white and black blocks to create uniform, smooth mantles, then split them in two, cut grooves in canyons rich in water below and, finally, left them in peace. For ages and ages.

And faced with nature's incredible workings, mankind could only bow in sacred awe.

Even the white men who came with the intention of taking over these lands, vanquishing everything and all those who crossed their conquering paths. Even those white men became convinced that this part of the Earth was too powerful for them to lay their hands on.

"Hey kids, do you realize this is one of the first parks ever created? It was opened in 1890."

The guide book tells us there are ancient forests that date back to the earliest human civilizations. From the signs posted near single trees, we discover that some of them are as old as Marco Polo or even Jesus Christ. The enormous, ashen sequoia tree trunks are so large that the thirty meter tall redwoods all around seem as flimsy and fragile as birches by comparison.

"Mum, try touching it… The bark is warm! And soft!"

The little one hugs a bit of warm, soft bark. His outline becomes a tiny dot on the gigantic surface of the sequoia. My eyes travel up the tree trunk, searching for the leaves. They are barely visible, so far from the ground; sprouting from a tree top so high it seems immeasurably narrower than the base.

Then I look down at the roots. As large as tree trunks, tens of them grab the earth, branching off from the enormous main body.

I think about the tree's age and the tiny outline of my son stuck to it. I think of its roots as they dig into the earth, charting time and force to a mystifyng power. And these are just the trees. Then come the rocks.

From the scenic spot where groups of visitors meet up fearing the altitude ("Please don't go near the edge, you know I'm frightened of heights!"), we see the geological eras blend into one another and rest, in memory of the past, mementos to the beginning of time.

Opposite us, beyond the dark valley full of trees, tourists are slowly climbing up to the peak. Teensy ants patiently making headway on weensy legs with colored jackets lost on the cliff side, walking up the multi-strata rock: every few thousand years having created a new wrinkle in the mountain's patient brow. It was there before and will be there still, in a dimension that swallows up all the ants —millions of previous ants and millions of future ones— venturing up right now.

"Excuse me, could you please take a picture of us?"

They hand me their camera and I take a portrait of the nice Asian couple, the mountains in the background.

The couple thanks me and walks away, mingling with the dozens of other tourists skipping on the rocks and striking poses, laughing down the lenses of other cameras.

Meanwhile I dwell upon us all, colored little ants, lost in these mountains.

Nothing. Our existence is a nothingness to be skipped on, laughed at and pictured. So vast, there is no point in even being frightened by it.

We take the car and drive nearby to the high ground of this valley. We park and get ready for the climb. I want to get to the top, look out from even higher up.

"Mum, what are you doing? Why are you taking your shoes off?"

"You try too, it's fantastic!"

I leave my shoes and take off.

"Wait for us, stop running!"

How can I not run? I have to go and skip around on the image of my nothingness.

I run along and drink the air. Continue running, panting, with long strides, towards the peak. And with a jump, presto! I leap off the tightrope I've been walking along for so many months, suspended over the canyon of dangers and fears: off and away.

I'm sprinting, my bare feet clinging to this large stone breast feeding the landscape, while lovingly looking out for the suckling human infants scrambling all over her. The wind brushes over both of us, pushes me on and carries away my ideas.

I reach the summit, swallowing my breath, throwing my gaze out. On the smooth peak, three thousand meters above the vast landscape resting below, and as far as my mind can see, I feel my fears, limits and misgivings slip away from the tips of my memories. I feel them flying, spreading over the outermost horizon and melting away in the crisp air.

CHAPTER V

First hurricane

The wind picks up and spreads out, chasing after itself, unconcerned by the obstacles, whistling, roaring, blowing and creaking. Fireplaces, railings, corners, leaves... Everything has come to life and is emitting sounds, enlivened by the wild wind.

The flashes of lightning rapidly carve white cuts through the black sky, then suddenly disappear into pitch darkness. Their sound follows a few seconds later: a sharp shriek of unruly energy blaring out for a fraction of time, then stretching out into a long, hollow roar. Laying in bed, we are jabbed by something fast pinching our brains and bodies, and hovering above us even when the thunder is over.

We hear the kids muttering from their bedrooms with their sleepless voices, but this time we don't try silencing or reassuring them.

"Don't worry, it's ok," I've tried telling them a few times already, sitting on the edge of a bed. But my voice was lost in a roar of thunder.

There's no point in trying to make myself heard: on this rumbling night, my words are but a soft whisper.

Especially after all the news reports: for days now, the newscasts, flashes and special reports have been showing pictures, maps and computer animated predictions of Hurricane Irene. They've shown it hitting the Lesser Antilles, Puerto Rico, the Dominican Republic, Haiti, Cuba, the Bahamas, Florida, South Carolina and North Carolina. Showing cataclysmic forecasts about it battering up the Atlantic coast inch by inch, saving nothing and no one; not even the cities that are normally unscathed by these catastrophic events such as Washington and New York.

Meanwhile, radio programs were often interrupted to update listeners on the shelters set up by the local authorities and remind people to stock up on food supplies and be prepared for long blackouts.

So, it's no wonder we are sleepless and jump at every clap of thunder and flash of lightning, whispering in the dark and expecting the worst, with weird pins and needles flowing through our bodies.

On the other hand, we could have turned the radio and television off once we'd received the essential updates; instead we let ourselves be trampled by the sights and sounds of catastrophic forecasts. We too wanted to hear the details, be struck by the buzz of a real emergency.

I walk to the window and try looking at the sky.

For several hours, it's been nursing heaps of clouds, turmoils of electric shocks and gigantic forges of drops and steam.

It's been screeching thunder and lightning halfway through the night and, now, it finally hatches a waterfall. So much water and wind you have to wonder which cosmic underbelly could possibly have held it all. Straight down, from the side, even up from below, apparently, as if the ground could vomit water upwards, in response to what the sky is pouring down.

The thunder, the kids and even our thoughts are dumb struck.

Only the house is whining, at times, as its wooden and plywood fibers are being bent by gusts so violent it feels like they're torturing it to see when it will give in.

I had stashed all the garden objects safely into the house the day before, to avoid them flying around breaking windows. Only the shrubs and tree tops give an idea of the strength of the wind. But they are barely visible because the darkness all round is the darkness of storms and, like a greedy babe, the water thirstily suckles all the light, leaving only a few flashes of lightning to illuminate the scenery for a few seconds at a time.

From the little I can see, in the flickers of lightning, the trees bend their heads, are shaken up and lose branches. But they are holding out.

My biggest fear during these storms is that one of the enormous trees in our garden or our neighbors' gardens will lose its strength and collapse onto our roof, crushing our house down on us.

I've always considered these large, old trees around us as dangerous enemies. Most of them are half dead: ivy suffocates their branches and trunks, leaving only a waft of leaves at the top proving they are actually alive.

All the trees around here are like that. With every gust of wind, they drop branches—as though they were ripe apples—down onto the electric cables, parked cars and driveway fences.

I've often wondered why, in this part of the world, they don't cut these great shrubs before building a house. I've even imagined buying a house in the area, repainting it, making it beautiful but, first of all, tearing down all the half dead trees around it.

However, on this night of furious groaning and labour, the distant flashes are illuminating the sky behind the trees, turning all those around me—alive, dry or half dead—into big, kind shadows.

They actually defuse the extremely strong wind, deviate the course of water, slow down the splashes here and there. Slapped by the storm, they surrender branches and leaves. I hear a whole one crashing down now, somewhere in the thick forest nearby. But they stand there, between us and the elements. Their open canopies get insulted by the turbulent newborn, even get bashed about and uprooted. But it's they who are hit, before the houses.

I think back to the images of hurricanes in the barren parts of the United States. Those houses torn apart leaving nothing, not even a load-bearing wall, a door frame or a chimney stack... Nothing. And there is nothing left anywhere nearby, around the house, as if all the devastated objects had been hauled away into outer space.

Where has it all ended up?

The unchallenged wind has hurled everything beyond every possible recon, torn bits who knows how far away and disintegrated them beyond recognition.

On the far side of the flat barren land, they may find the first remains in the nearest woodland.

A slap of light hits the treetops rocked by the wind. They bend over, their leaves whirring rapidly. Then darkness again, the wind whistling and moaning in gusts.

Those houses flying apart in the hurricanes are like ours, made of plywood and plaster. Here they call it drywall but it's still just plaster and plywood.

Seeing them in the movies, these sort of houses seemed solid mansions. I imagined them resting on stone or brick walls, strengthened by wood, iron or concrete beams. But now that I'm living in one, I've discovered the truth: drywall houses seem to have been built by the little carpenter pig. The one whose house the wolf blew down with just a few extra huffs and puffs.

You can't hang shelves, paintings or heavy coat racks in these American houses. Once we had a leaking pipe and panicked at the idea of having to break into the wall for god knows how long and how much money. Instead, we discovered that the plumber, happily whistling his way, simply sawed out a little section, repaired the pipe, put the section back and all was done. He took off whistling and we were left looking at the small section of sawed wall, in disbelief.

All American houses have this feature, and not only the houses, practically all buildings. All the malls, offices, schools, hospitals, supermarkets and hotels: they all seem a bit counterfeit, quickly put together. Beautiful on the surface but assembled at top speed and held together by spit and duct tape. Looking closely, deluxe materials turn out to be fake marble, fake wood, even fake brick. And carpeting everywhere, linoleum and super thin wood panelling. Two-ply on top of panels, covering battens that quickly become worn down.

I'd always imagined America as sturdy and shiny. Everything new, glossed over and sheened. Instead I now see scaling, holes, mould and peeling corners everywhere.

A clap of thunder pulls me out of my thoughts about building materials. The rain, lashing down on the walls and the roof, is yelling at me: look at me, only me, me, me...

Throwing the bossy water a challenge, I turn my back and walk away from it—spoiled brat, always claiming more. Stepmother Nature's botched childbed.

Who knows whether the trees will actually defend us? I don't know if there is any scientific proof they will. But I cling to the thought of those shadows and their canopies spreading out between the houses, patiently enduring the downpour. Thinking of them as our guardians, I manage to shout out one last: "Go to sleep, there's nothing to be afraid of!" pull the sheet up to my chin and wait for dawn.

Downgraded

The hurricane never actually reached Washington. It became weary after all those days of yelling and threatening, building up and spitting out monstrous water creatures. It travelled north, furiously clawing the land, trampling houses and pulling up poles, roofs and plants. Smothering and killing people and animals; invading fields and ruining crops. But during all this stretching north, with surges of cruelty and devastation, it finally lost energy and wore itself out.

As it approached Maryland, Virginia and the District, Irene was downgraded to tropical storm, like so many others. And the damages amounted to the usual cables torn by fallen branches, a few roofs knocked in by uprooted trees, a handful of cars swerving across the road hitting other cars, and other trivial accidents.

It's the second time in the last few months that Washington is left unscathed by nature's great devastating performances. While we were still traveling through California, there had been an earthquake which had jerked the city's underbelly quite a bit. Reports showed people being bucked up and down, everything being thrown in the air and landing back in its place, over and over again. Powerless people screeching in fear, their howls sounding like someone suddenly realizing the grim insignificance of his existence on this great self-ruling sphere.

Laying aside the fears and inconveniences, the biggest damage created by the wild fault lines were the cracks in the symbolic obelisk. Raised in the mid 1800s to honor George Washington, it stands in the middle of the city, surrounded by all the most important buildings, and, by law, no other construction can be taller than it, not even in the more distant surroundings. Which explains the absence of skyscrapers we noticed when we first landed.

And now, after the earthquake, the enormous monument, the

geographic crux of the American empire, is slightly cracked and has been closed to the public.

A matter of little significance, surely. But with a bit of malice and some creative Italian metaphorical thinking, one could strike an analogy with the stature of the most powerful country in the world nowadays.

But that's not happening here, from what I see. Here they have taken the usual poised pragmatic approach: the obelisk is closed to tourists, and that's that.

A year has now gone by

Looking outside, I realize a scenario I've already seen is now repeating itself.

A glimmer of autumn is slipping into nature. It's not a visible change yet, everything is still green and strong. Millions of leaves are shining in the light, while animals skip around, call out and run after food. Nonetheless... summer is dwindling. The prevailing vital force which was flying around in a hurry and shining over everything, is starting to slow down. The sun skims the roofs of these low-rise houses earlier in the evening. Before even having dinner, we're already feeling like getting home, resting and looking out from within.

And the feeling is no longer foreign or taking me by surprise, it's rather like a well-known friend gliding towards me. The first repetition of a cycle starting over.

"A year's gone by already. Have you noticed?"

A year since we shed Rome and our old life, and we flew over the ocean, naked, ready to see and try out new things.

My travel companion looks out the window.

"I'll go move the car, there's a lot of wind and it could be hit by a branch."

A year has gone by and the amazement has ceased.

That's what has happened every time we have lived through all the seasons of a new destination.

Here in the States we had summer, autumn, winter and spring. In Africa, it was the dry season and rainy season. In the Middle East, the different degrees of heat and dryness.

Seasons we took in for the first time, covered us with new smells and sounds, new textures and tastes. Unfiltered sensations, to be absorbed with our mouths, hands and eyes open wide. Trying to understand the new community we were in, watching how it viewed the world, which customs it would roll out with every new season, the clothes it wore at each different occasion... And every now and then, sampling a new outfit ourselves.

"I can smell the rain coming."
My husband comes back in and unwraps the newspaper someone throws in our driveway every morning.
"I hadn't picked it up yet."
I watch him open the pages and concentrate on his reading.
On the last page, there's a big ad for a chimney sweeping service. Better get ahead, the ad says, we'll be lighting our chimneys soon. They're right after all, so I make a mental note of this other thing that needs to be done. Well, that's the way it goes, every time. The cycle comes full circle and everything sorts itself out. We rearrange our impressions, classify our sensations as they happen and, finally, recognize them. We align our choices and our habits with the civilization we are now part of. And voilà, we are no longer castaways, rather integrated expats, properly dressed and shod.

That evening, the notion that a year has gone by is picked up again around the dinner table and lots of comments gush out.
"Hey, this time last year we were still sleeping on the floor, on lilos, remember?"
"One year ago, we had no idea where we were."
"We didn't know where to go shopping."
"They didn't want to sell us a car because we didn't have a credit history and they didn't trust us."
"We didn't know how the petrol stations worked."
"We couldn't understand what people were saying."
"We didn't know how health insurance worked."

"Remember when..." comes up again and again in the following days. At the start of this new work and school year, every gesture shimmers with mild, satisfied happiness: the feeling of slipping one's life on again, like a familiar and comfortable old glove.

"Is the school bus schedule still the same, Mum?"

"Yes, and at the same spot."

"My classmate, the one who lives near here, will also be taking it this year."

The time for awkwardness and improvisations is over: we can start establishing our own routines. Brick upon brick of new habits which soon stop being new and reassure our morale that, here too, we are finding our way among these people, anchoring ourselves in their same rituals, attitudes and bearings.

The school bus stops and opens its doors. The driver's usual wave, my greeting, his half smile and the doors closing again behind the kids.

I drive home, down roads and past garden corners, the plants and parking lots now greeting me, recognizing me and making me feel at home. And I move about with renewed casualness.

I think about the fact we mirror ourselves in our habits.

As if the mental image we have of ourselves were to blow up and spread out, bits of it landing on everything around us. When we walk along, these bits of ourselves which have settled on things, shine back and we can identify them. Like a trade mark lighting up as we go by. But only we can see them, because it is our very own. Telling us *that* thing now belongs to us and has become part of our story line.

It's a warm day, so I grab the trowel and some little plants and start digging holes in the front garden.

"The last flowers of the season, eh?" the neighbor opposite comments with a smile while I transfer plants from pot to flower bed.

"I was thinking: I'd really like to learn some Italian," she adds as I stand up and shake the dirt off. "My husband and I are retired and we travel a lot, we really love Italy."

And I reply that I would love to teach her. I'm available for lessons: schedule and fees are flexible. "I'm part of an Italian networking group, could that interest you?" I add. "We have interesting projects, a reading group, we put together events… I can sign you up straight away, if you want!"

"That would be great!" my neighbor yells back clapping her hands in a show of enthusiasm I've never seen in Italy but encounter quite often here.

I raise my gloved hand and smile as my neighbor goes back inside. A trace of her happiness, although slightly over the top and contrived, has made its way into me too. We really should all make more of an effort and show more enthusiasm, I decide, and throw a keen "Hello!" to the well kept old man who walks down the street every day, slowly dragging along his two fat dachshunds.

Did he hear me?

I put the tools away, get changed and set off to meet an acquaintance.

I drive along, my clear gaze looking out over the roads, houses, large avenues with traffic lights and the lower buildings of the commercial area.

The places I go to all the time. I like walking through this part of town because it has a European feel to it.

Since the 80s, the New Urbanism movement, respectful of human needs, has been reconsidering and recreating our ancient urban style in various parts of the US. Which is like what they had in old American towns: a space where homes and shops, offices, restaurants, benches and squares were all mixed up together, creating spaces where people could mingle, meet and get together. It will never be like that again; the ancient cities were built from scratch with these principles in mind. Nowadays, areas of this kind are just accessories in wealthy neighborhoods with a well educated population, designed to bring comfort. Or, in degraded areas, experiments attempting to re-introduce a certain degree of civic life.

It's really too bad that in Italy, instead, all the new neighborhoods are being based on opposite principles, modern American ideas: places to live over here and commercial centers over there; bigger and bigger industrial and artisanal areas, medical and financial centres, set further and further apart, both inconvenient and inhospitable.

Why is it that in the country I come from, we never seem to believe we have something worth exporting, apart from bags and shoes, machineries, a few medical excellencies and a handful of genius discoveries? We always seem to consider our traditions and lifestyle unappealing, requiring change. Forgetting that, in other parts of the world, they are actually being studied and replicated.

And wouldn't it be best to mix up traditions and blend attitudes in other fields too? That's what comes to mind, soon after, watching the dismayed expression of my lunchtime companion: a young Italian mother with a little boy in an American nursery school. A child at her son's nursery was expelled because he lifted the girls' skirts. The teachers considered his behavior disrespectful and detrimental to the dignity of the girls in the class.

"And it didn't end there," the young lady adds, her eyes goggling. "After that incident, letters were sent to all the parents explaining that the kids were no longer allowed to exchange little love notes, even on Valentine's Day."

"Five year olds writing love notes?"

"You know, little notes saying 'Tommy loves Jenny' and stuff of the kind."

Which provide hours of chuckling, bitterness and mooning over at all ages. OK, the notes don't help them concentrate, whether in nursery school or senior high school. But that's not what the educators in this school are worried about. They're worried about the interest, the awakening of an impulse ("God forbid!"), being already so strong in a five-year old.

And when kids play out their natural instinct with little sex games, the grown-ups' worry and concern are hidden behind iron-clad justifications: "We are expelling him to defend the girls' dignity. To teach everyone that being a girl doesn't mean being at the mercy of boys' desires."

Who could possibly be so bold as to contradict them? Or question whether their irrefutable arguments are not actually hiding a prurient attitude, or deep-set awkwardness, when faced with nature's spontaneous sexual drive?

I tell the young mother I find this civilization deeply contradictory.

Even nudity in statues and paintings is cause for embarrassment, blushing and giggling: when I accompanied my son on a field trip to the National Gallery, entire class groups covered their eyes in shame while walking past the works of art of the Renaissance! From puberty onwards, people become obsessed with hiding their bodies from sight, including the eyes of parents and doctors. And I sometimes have to stop myself from laughing as a doctor makes me wrap up in layers of gowns, clothes and bandages to then uncover the minute part he has to examine.

On the other hand, the way people dress and behave is quite laid back, and having sex almost seems like a casual diversion: a healthy physical activity one can find the time for between the gym and a board meeting. Even in books and on television, in movies and song lyrics… The relationship between men and women is open, explicit, standardized. There's hardly any room for fun, and no seduction whatsoever.

So I find my own answer: "Maybe that's how this contradiction works! If sex is so embarrassing, then it must be made harmless, unthreatening. Initially, it must be censured then, when it becomes unavoidable, it must be approached as if it were just any other mild, ordinary activity."

"Poor kid," the young mother continues. "How will he make it through school from now on? With this stain on his record, his parents breathing down his neck, his new teachers mistrusting him… He's going to become a rapist when he grows up. And everyone will say: 'No wonder, he already had weird tendencies when he was a kid.' And do you know what makes me really angry? This is all happening in a country where the biggest TV show is a kind of Miss Italy for tiny kids. You know the one I mean."

Yes, I know it. The talent show full of made up and decked out little girls, dolled up like little Barbies. Sometimes they have nervous breakdowns, their extremely young nerves snap, crushed by their strung out parents who are so eager to show them off, make them shine and be coveted by everyone out there.

"Who's protecting their dignity? Their womanhood is traded in the saddest, most *cliché* manner. But since it's become a commodity, it's ok."

I say goodbye to the Italian mother and drive home. The little boy's story has left me slightly baffled, but I find myself nonetheless smiling and relaxed while driving through the neighborhood.

There is always something off-key out there. Now, this country's strange habits and its different sensitivity, don't feel so odd any longer. My brain takes them in and files them in the "new and quirky" folder which is already quite consistent and constantly being stocked.

The sense of adventure is over, and with it the feeling of sailing through uncharted waters, eyes goggling in disbelief. I'm sticking to the shoreline. My journey is now made up of free thoughts and a simple life, curiosity and the longing to explore: what can I actually do around here? How does this glove fit and what can it grasp…?

The torch

A few days later, I'm at another lunch date. This time in one of those cafés of a chain offering fast, light meals, with everyone sitting at big, long tables; the perfect place for people to mingle. Although they all look so busy, I doubt they'll actually meet anyone new.

My new acquaintance is also typing away at her iPhone while waiting for me. Perfectly integrated in the hardworking American atmosphere and society which she, like many others, has chosen to climb by making money and becoming successful.

I look at my hands which are dirty from gardening, again. I wonder about all those openings I don't even know I'm missing while living in the land of opportunity.

Ever since I started traveling, I've developed my own freedom of expansion. Quitting my job and sedentary life has taught me to move around and explore all sorts of possibilities. Embark on projects, pick up or walk away from opportunities, miss boats, catch shooting stars… But never anything well defined, structured or certified.

Practically all the clients are busy working hard, hooked to the wi-fi connection. Students from the nearby university, researchers from nearby research centers, businessmen, lawyers, teachers.

The place is big. There's even room for a few mums with little kids and friends chatting away. But the overlaying buzz and tech hub industriousness, can be put down to the customers with their laptops open on the table, deep in thought, hooking up and streaming along the connection's various currents.

And while my new acquaintance is describing the established American milestones which ferry keen citizens through degrees to PhDs and careers, the question buzzing around my head lands, annoyingly, like a fly on my salad plate: "Where do I stand in all this?"

The famous torch-bearing statue wanders around the States, sauntering into crowded eateries and ambling through customers. She's looking for those who don't take full advantage of the wonderful freedom she represents.

Lured by awkwardness, she finds it between the folds of excuses. She unveils it, strikes it and highlights it with her beacon.

I'm telling my acquaintance that, every few years, my life is scoured by the re-assignment sponge, stopping me from ever building anything long term or engaging. And, I have to admit, my roaming existence actually fits some traits of my character like a glove: a mind with slightly itchy feet, holding commitment on a leash as if it were a nosy, restless puppy, who's never had its full.

That's when the torch reaches me. Leans over me and finds it: my awkwardness in not being among those who actively generate or receive a tangible compensation. It was just sitting there silently, in the corner, ashamed of itself. And is now being thrown into the spotlight.

My throat tightens, coughs up a piece of vegetarian sandwich and I drink a sip of water to rein it in.

"Oh, I've got to go! They're waiting for me at the office," my acquaintance says, without having noticed.

She collects her things and stands up, her mind already generating.

My awkwardness instead remains, kneeling in the middle of the room, covering its face with its hands.

I accompany the busy professional out of the eatery, watch her quickly slip into her car and drive out of one of those typical big American parking spots.

I walk on towards my car and suddenly neat structures appear before my eyes: the roads are just straight lines, houses just cubes, trees just cylinders with jagged tops. Just meaningless shapes.

No one is expecting me, anywhere…

Living these moments is part of the country-changing challenge: looking around and suddenly feeling my world is incredibly empty. Surrounded by shapes and geometrical figures. Meaningless frames.

The roads, houses and places I go don't have a message for me, they don't tell me who I am or what I should do. They're not there for a reason. They're just empty containers, uselessly shining in the sun.

It's up to me, each time, to replenish these containers with meaning, emotions, fulfillment. A sort of reverse house moving: I have to fill the large empty boxes around me with purpose and significance.

I walk past my car and direct my steps towards the University. A hexahedron of windows and red brick which a small, colorful swarm of students enter and exit. Their books under their arms, biting down on their determination. Pirates hounding for a job, they'll soon have to jump aboard a ship of opportunity and strong arm their way until they become gainful and grasp their own fate, their loot, with their own hands.

The road is lined with tall trees which, slowly, before my eyes, stop resembling plain shapes. I start seeing slightly lighter bark on the long branches and the first leaves turning to gold. I see the beginnings of a warm, full autumn. Notice a spree of loose, soft feelings strolling along beside me. Distinguish the need to leave the past behind and foster a change, seize on peaceful habits to pursue something new.

I quickly go back to my car, as if going home meant going towards something. And my mind is beaming with new questions.

So, America, what can I fill you with? What am I to place in these shapes I have around me?

And while my car takes me towards some new beginning, I feel the cool breeze prickling the air and plants exuding smells and full colors. I feel life promising me new routes and joyful itineraries.

And yet (second hurricane)

Autumn is here so it's time to pull out the besom and get to work, again.

Raking the leaves, straightening up the garden furniture, sawing and stacking the fallen branches with the fire wood.

I notice that some neighbors stack their fallen branches on the edge of the road for the sanitation trucks to collect.

They all have fireplaces around here. At least one in every home. The smell of burning wood tickles the streets with a warm essence of rest and relaxation. So why get rid of the branches the trees have stripped themselves of? They burn perfectly well, we have used them several times.

Maybe they have a gas fireplace, or an electric one, or maybe it just isn't what one does. Maybe, here again, in this part of the world, they just want to follow the rules: firewood is to be bought from the specialized dealer, cut into regular pieces and tidily stacked.

I did the same, early on in the season. I bought a big stack of wood from two lumberjacks from Virginia selling logs door to door. Both very thin, wearing worn clothes which had taken on the colors of the woods, they jumped lightly on and off their rusty pickup truck. Father and son, their movements perfectly in sync: throwing one another logs from the pickup truck to the ground, it took them a few minutes to stack them all tightly along half of our garage wall.

And, while raking the leaves in the garden, I often come across some of those little branches that fall to the ground with the slightest gust. And I end up throwing them away with everything else, just to not waste time.

But I realize that in these polluted times, even just lighting a fireplace is pleasantly selfish. So now, every time I don't collect the wood fallen from the sky, I feel guilty. The trees have stripped themselves and offered them to me by the handful, throwing them away seems rude and disrespectful.

My brother-in-law regards my neighbors' and my waste of wood emblematic. He compares it to the devastating impact of American consumerism on the planet's fragile equilibrium.

The brother-in-law arrived a few days ago, with the typical sharp mind and perceptive vision visitors always have. He shakes his head as he strolls down the street watching smoke curling out of the chimneys. In the lanes of a big supermarket, he wanders around grimly pointing out the sizes of the products: bottles of medicines as big as buckets, bags of sweets the size of a suitcase, soft drinks that could quench Gargantua's thirst…

"This planet has no future, it's over!" he comments.

On other occasions, he observes the constant flow of traffic, in both directions, along the countless six lane highways, at all times of day and night. And boilers constantly lit, the overheating, the drafts blowing through drywall homes, the drywall itself…

"To think I wake up at dawn to sort out my recycling bins, regularly turn lights off, save water… It's all useless. There's no future."

I too am mindful, and shake my head. Siding with his worries, however, I avoid aggravating them by underlining the fact that the United States obtain half of their enormous energy intake from fossil fuels. They are among the world's most callous smokers: gathering the dirtiest and most primitive energy reserves and exhaling them out into the Earth's face.

The latest alternative they have developed over the last few years is shale gas. A gas extracted from certain kinds of underground rock formations with a procedure producers say is eco-friendly. Environmentalists instead say it's harmful because it wrecks landscapes and pollutes water tables, devastating whole regions.

Following my brother-in-law's visit, I briefly endorse his idea that environmental zeal is useless. I take it on and nourish the awareness that millions of people on the American and Asian continents are happily burning the earth's stability, refusing to sign agreements and denying evidence. I accept it, feed it and tuck it up tightly in blankets of dismay.

Then, a few months after our dreaded hurricane, I find myself watching the images of the terrible gales in Liguria and, in early November, the most devastating of them all, in Genova, killing six people.

No one had foreseen its magnitude and, most of all, no one had given enough notice. Far from the paranoid media outpouring which is set into motion in situations of the kind over here: the gale in Genova had simply been announced, not demonized, so everyone had been caught off guard while going about their daily business instead of being already locked up inside, hoping damages would be minimal.

On the internet, I see images of roads and houses, cars and people, chastened by the deluge. Everyman's negligence befalling them: those roads, those people. Martyrs of bad weather. Sacrificial victims in a rite that grants no atonement.

I watch the dark outline of a man walking through the high water, his arms grappling the air, grasping for a meaning as well as a handhold. But he finds neither and the bubbling, muddy tide drags him away, suddenly weightless and insignificant, his arms still swaying in the air.

Is this really what is in store for our planet? A constant, full-blown ordeal, nature shaking and scratching humans off its back, as if it were a mangy dog?

Baffled by all the images and questions, I turn my computer off. Looking at an empty screen can sometimes help to focus and make important decisions.

Such as turning off lights—which I had lit for companionship rather than necessity—tearing up old notes before carefully throwing them into the proper recycling bin, and turning down the heating. Such as going into the garden and picking up even the tiniest fallen branches.

Soon after, the wind changes tack.
Vague whirls of fate start swelling up.
They flow over the body's continents and surrounding waters. Getting tied up and winding round, shaping new conditions, and a threat.

Each medical check up confirms traces which call for more tests which, in turn, require more tests. Until, one day, the young specialist squints at me and points out the results:

"It could be anything, from very serious to nothing at all. We can't tell yet."

I'm already wiped out.

"Do you really have no idea? Based on your experience, other clinical cases, similar situations…"

The young specialist shakes her head.

"I really can't tell."

It all sounds like a broken record: my body, again, hostage to the same dangers as a few months ago, in another nook of tissue.

I wanted to pursue new experiences, take advantage of my fitting in, travel down new roads… Instead, I'm trapped, caught up in the path set by medical procedures and growing concerns.

Soon after, both of these become magnified when the suit-and-tie doctor facing us seems upset he hasn't set off any alarm bells in my eldest daughter: she is unabashed, actually smiling kindly.

"I believe you may not have understood, your condition could be very serious."

He's not wearing a white coat because he wants to be cool, his patient's buddy. Then again, he almost looks pleased as if he couldn't wait to direct a young girl's attention to one of life's dark, icy recesses.

"Don't worry, you know they always like to exaggerate things here," I tell her once we are outside.

"I know, Mum, don't worry."

"The important thing is not to listen. I'm sure everything's fine."

Not to listen… Really?

Staying home is what such a situation calls for. With my head stuck between four drywalls, instead of out there, embarking on projects. Back home, to watch my dismay trying to plug the doors and windows and salvage the things I love. But it's too late: the storm has hit and nothing can be saved this time. There's no point in trying to rescue the pieces by bringing them inside because that's where the mother eye of all storms has broken out: inside the room, inside the body, inside the mind which is mulling over the problem.

In the super strong drywall little house, the piglet's house which made it through the hurricanes… It's now harboring these internal tornadoes. Whirlwinds bending and cracking everything, twisting every ray of light and every sound.

The new alarm bells make us parents move, confusedly, in the dark, fearsome storm.

They make me feel like a weary lioness as I take my daughter to the doctors: I can do nothing to protect her, nothing to help her, just smile.

They force me to go home with a show of optimism that is wearing me out and I fear I won't be able to hold out much longer.

Her tests and mine overlapping, on my desk and in my mind.

At night, my hands travel, my fingertips seeking the touch of another skin, wanting to brush up to something that will confirm we are still here and haven't been kidnapped by dark forces.

But after so many years of certainty, and contact which smoothly transferred warmth from one hand to the other, my fingers now find a cold emptiness that stings.

My companion is lost, faraway.

Who knows what routes he's been traveling along while I was busy with my latest discoveries and my adventures in this new land. As I ploughed through recent perils. Where was he?

Only now do I see the distance, become aware of the job paths, projects, experiences and encounters which have turned out to be his alone.

Only now do I have the strength to look into his eyes as they avert their gaze from mine.

Strolling through the same old empty neighborhood, I suddenly find it to be full of what's been thrown out of my life. Children playing with their dad as he focuses on scoring a three-pointer, family cars coming home from work and peacefully parking in the driveways, smoke and voices rising from backyard barbecues with friends, couples walking hand in hand, at the end of the day, into the sunset. I watch them and take them with me as I wander home, where nothing belongs to me any more.

I too try to conjure them up again, between us. Why are they no longer?

But all I manage to fire up are palaver, tactics and arguments. Nothing is working, the same useless MOs repeating themselves, over and over again.

A friendly face appears on the computer screen.

"So, are you thinking of coming back to Italy? Maybe a break would do you good."

"I've got more medical exams and we're right in the middle of the school year."

School is full on, plus homework, dance lessons, piano lessons, classmates... Kids' feelings are propped up by so many things. Sensitive, important and complex, I can't derail them just to catch a breath of fresh air in Italy.

My parents are also fragile entities by now, perceptive and suspicious. They have a hard time keeping their own health concerns at bay, and are already starting to worry about my marriage. I can't just turn up with my bagfuls of need for comfort.

"No, I really can't."

So I stay, stuck in my thick, grey solitude. No longer a sensation I feel as I wander through unknown places, rather a dull pain I carry into my own home.

My own body parts are estranged from one another, as are my thoughts and my deepest feelings.

Like a puzzle falling apart, loose bits of a mechanism now incapable of serving its purpose.

I wonder how the house will manage to stay standing, and how long for. When will it keel over and the drywall come apart, like a splintered coffin, flooding the garden, road and woods with the bleak wind blowing inside it?

Luckily, the house sits tight while the hurricane festers. It can't be opened with a can opener, nor can the partitions and people inside be exposed to the wholesome impact of plants.

Whereas I can, and I do, very often. I throw myself into the woods again. It's easy here, they're everywhere. Just a few meters from my house, I'm already on a lane leading to a public park and, further on, to a pathway along a stream through the shrubs.

I often walk through these woods of gentle giants. Partly covered in ivy, partly blown down by the storms, but mostly still tall, old and mighty. They are yellow and wise at this time of year, the blue sky and strong light peeping through the leaves.

Walking among them, the breadth of my sensations stretches out, and stretches again, until it becomes wide open. A vast, spotless land which hurricanes blow over and leave behind, with nothing holding them back or fueling them on further.

Because everything else is an empty container and filling it with meaning requires a big effort. Whereas nature is there, all around, full and thriving, with its own meaning and no need for anything else. No effort is required, I can just grab it by the handful.

And that's where memories can resurface, shine again through the countless branches. The memories of distant years. With my companion. Tuscan landscapes travelled in an embrace, our voices enlaced with the flames in the fireplace, life choices made walking, smiling, through nature. A friendly time, flowing gently like spring sunshine on naked skin. Days marked by a peaceful intensity: being the way we wanted each other to be. Ruled by no one and nothing else. Telling one another what we wished to forge together, without holding back.

The light breaks away from the objects, skims my head and slides into my thoughts. It pushes my gaze upwards, towards the autumn-hemmed leaves high up, poised above all solitude, rustling with life.

The first dry leaves make the ground crunch under my feet. It's a cheerful banter, as if commenting on my passing and laughing at this weird plant moving around and making noise.

Wouldn't it be nice to be like a plant. Part of nature, full of vigor and meaning.

Suddenly it all becomes clear.

There's no point in leaving, this time, that's for sure. I don't need to reconnect with my motherland tissue, don't want to find loving words and reassuring motions. I don't need anyone right now. I can't be reached by help, therefore I don't depend upon it.

I'll do what is required, without squandering my energy or boosting any storms. I'll neatly stack and tie my problems onto a small raft—as far away as possible from my feelings—and ferry them to a shore of solutions.

And a gust of gratitude lifts my sensations. It hoists the skirts of dismay, which suddenly runs away, ashamed.

For once in my lifetime, I will have lived in this country not to find a job or seek apparent gratifications, rather to seize vigor from isolation and temper my courage on the example of others.

To understand that solutions come from within, not from without.

And slowly, the winds become lighter.

From the core of my mind, at the heart of the room in our little house, gentle flurries of hope swirl up, followed by outcomes and quiet healing.

The drywall and everything inside turns out to be sturdier than I thought. Patient and compassionate, it lies in wait as the mist clears and the dust settles.

The safe, white, elderly, wise house stands solid and clear while the wounded tissues within it are healed. Our hands can finally find and grasp one another.

Our eyes can meet once again.

The same old tune

It's almost Christmas.

I don't know how I got here; I must have lost track of time while the hurricanes were melting away.

We hadn't considered going back to Italy—too expensive and such a hassle. Also, we still hadn't received all the feedback which eventually told my daughter and me that all was well. Plus, she was still recovering from a small operation. So, no, we hadn't thought about taking off.

"Great, we can enjoy a white American Christmas!"
"With a log burning in the fireplace and snow falling."
"Christmas songs and decorations everywhere."

The whole family cheers at the prospect of living this holiday in the States.

And we discover they really go overboard with both music and decorations, over here. Songs are constantly being played over every radio and in all public places. They echo in your head and you, your neighbors, friends and family end up whistling the same tunes all day long. An explosion of traditional songs—always the same ones—plus a few recent hits which soon sound old from hearing them so often.

I'm not sure, but I don't think it's the same in Italy. I'd never noticed the constant emphasis on Christmas tunes where I come from. Here instead it's an obsession. It feels like living in a Walt Disney cartoon, with Mickey and Minnie walking down decorated streets with Jingle Bells playing over and over again.

And the decorations are absolutely everywhere. Not only street lights paid for by the shopkeepers wanting to attract a few more customers, like in Italy. Here, it's a competition between neighbors as to who strings the most colored lights on their hedges, has the largest shower of white lights falling from their gutters, the vastest stretch of fireflies on the bare tree trunks and the best shaped reindeer, present or sledge lights in their garden; and gigantic red bows on front doors, evergreen garlands on fences, even wreaths hanging from car bonnets.

"Can we do it too? Can we put up decorations?"
"Of course we can!"

That's why we stayed: to live the occasion the American way. So, in the following days, we adapt to the local traditions.

Our Christmas tree reaches the ceiling (then again ceilings are low here, about two and a half meters, so it's not a gigantic tree) and it's so full of balls, bows and lights that some branches bend down, graciously surrendering to the ground.

"I think we've put enough decorations on it."
"Let's do the outdoor ones now!"

We wouldn't dream of going against their wishes, and actually hurry to comply. Partly to feel the thrill of conforming and connecting with the neighbors wearing duffle coats and red noses, who watch us as we stretch outlandish amounts of lights in the garden, and call out joyful greetings. Just like when they see us gardening, throwing a baseball or washing our car. People on the street hail an enthusiastic "How's it going?" as a sort of acknowledgement or badge: you're doing the same things I do, therefore you are part of my community; I greet you and thereby affirm we both belong to a common good.

But that's not the main reason why we went outdoors, into the cold wind, to numb our hands on the hedges and railings, in the dim light that is struggling to make its way through grey layers of unbroken sky getting darker by the minute.

It's above all because of the dark layer which every afternoon and earlier each day, buries even the closest of objects into invisible, far corners. You'd want to don a crown of candles in the evening and wander around begging for light to come back.

Lately however, as the dusk tingles our skin with an almost bothersome dismay, some stretches of the long, silent roads are overtaken by the lively relief of Christmas lights. Some of them are timed to light up as the sun sets, whereas others are lit at different hours by diligent neighbors. Creating small pit stops for eyes in search of something.

We too now want to do our bit to soothe the dismay of all wayfarers.

We wander in the total darkness, the last meters of lights in hand, and hurriedly scatter them around in erratic sweeps. Then we plug them in and revel in our handiwork which is creating a nice, slightly anarchic, dazzling effect. What will the others think of it? They may consider our work of art a sight for sore eyes seeing as their lights follow strict designs, all symmetry and uniformity...

Whether they have appreciated or been annoyed, the neighbors come up our drive a few days later to sing Christmas carols. They ring the bell, and as soon as I open the front door, they start playing (one kid on a trumpet, another on a sax) and singing (younger kids resembling a small professional choir) some Christmas classics. The same ones that have been played over the radio, in every public space, etc. over the last few weeks.

I'm so surprised I'm joyfully glued to the doorstep. Enchanted, I hug my arms around myself to keep warm.

The cartoon has come to life, taken on the human form of our neighbors and reached our front door to include us too...

I finally get a grip of myself and rally the family.

"Hey, guys! Come and see!"

The girls come straight down, their faces gleaming with curiosity. The little one instead is missing—they tell me he buried himself in the most hidden corner of the basement as soon as he heard the doorbell.

Maybe I should have him exorcised...

The sisters and I—and a few moments later, my husband home from work—delight in the show, with expressions of vibrant Christmas cheer, neighborly love and harmony stuck to our faces.

The neighbors, seeing our rapture, sing on, song after song.

The very same withdrawn neighbors who had surprised us with cookies when we had arrived but then disappeared behind thick curtains of privacy. The noiseless ones we never see and never hear—with five kids we never see and never hear—and always worry we're not liked by, can't understand or can't be understood by. They are now all here, with another neighbor and a few of her kids, all together, smiling, playing and singing for us...

As soon as they finish, we obviously insist upon them all coming in to show them our tree and our creche.

And they do all come in; slightly stiff, on tenterhooks. They come in, look around, and sing a few more songs, seeing as they're at it. This time, we too allow our Christmas spirit to pour out in tuneful add-ons to their wonderfully assembled performance.

And then it's finally time to loosen up, sit down, maybe even have a glass of something and joyfully exchange glances for a moment. It's the happy ending with the ice breaking, the continents drifting closer and me becoming, at last, friends with the neighbors. Maybe.

"Would you like a glass of Prosecco? A cup of tea? A slice of panettone, a juice for the kids?"

Instead the usual recoiling sets in, the usual quick pulling out, the usual even bigger smile to say no, thank you, we really have to go.

"Please, make yourselves comfortable, let's have a chat, I can light the fire."

"No, thank you. Thank you again."

The door closes on the whiff of pipe dreams walking out, with the neighborhood carolers, and I cross my arms.

"It's chilly."

"What's for dinner?"

This daughter is always hungry, going through a staggering growing phase, with a merry appetite for life and constantly needing food. I send her off to flush out her brother and make my way to the kitchen to cook dinner.

"You'll have to wait a bit, we've got guests coming tonight."

Meanwhile I ponder the fact I'm still misunderstanding, even after being here more than a year. I still haven't learnt to tell things apart; in my brain, common courtesy go hand in hand with warm-heartedness. Here instead, they don't.

The latter doesn't seem to be an essential element of this country's spirit. Whereas there seems to be an abundance of the former, rooted in all fundamental behaviors: standing united and feeling part of the community to reassure each other we are Americans, in tune with the homeland and its rules.

All this has its unquestionable appeal: feeling so strongly about the handful of signature traditions which anchor you to everyone else.

"I hadn't expected it, before getting here," I find myself commenting, that night, at the dinner table.

I explain that I'm surprised the Americans among whom I find myself living, have so eagerly founded their existence on such a small, solid fulcrum of traditions.

They feel strongly for these moments of collective intent, with everyone behaving exactly the same way and in the same spirit. They create them, respect them, live them with passionate concern. Every national holiday and Sunday morning in church (of whatever denomination), as well as the School BBQs, Halloween Costumes, Thanksgiving Turkeys and Christmas Lights…

It's a race between neighbors as to who will perform these rituals in the most accurate and heartfelt manner. The outdoor decorations, the right greeting addressed in the right tone of voice to whoever you meet, the dress codes, states of mind and above all the purchases: everything complies to the common intent, everyone agreeing to do the same thing, at the same time.

It's almost unbelievable. Fabulous, in some ways.

Something a whole nation can grow around and impose upon others, believing so much in itself as to become an example for all—*urbi et orbi*[6].

"Ok, but don't you think your observations are related to the social circle you live in?" a dinner guest suggests.

Sure. After all, we are living in these very white protestant neighborhoods. Residential suburbs for families who base their existence on everything white and protestant and familiar. Including the need to all live together, in a circle, around the bonfire of their traditions.

"And this neighborhood is so WASP," another dinner guest adds. "Did you know that, until a few decades ago, even Italians were not welcome here? All catholics in fact."

Because every community, at its origins, establishes its own rules: in this case, the exclusion of Italians and all catholics.

Then, in a typically obstinate American way, a catholic lawyer decided he wanted to live right here, in this very neighborhood.

Being American, stubborn and a lawyer—and because Americans are incredibly capable of creating the most unbelievable situations to then, remarkably, make them disappear—the stubborn, catholic lawyer won a few lawsuits, managed to buy a plot of land and build his house on it.

Laws were then passed to prohibit rules that were overtly racist towards any ethnic or religious group, opening the road for the intrusion of catholics and Italians which continued, on and off, to this day.

"However," I add, "just like the other Italians and catholics living here, we don't disrupt their traditions."

We are used to mimicry: we travel and adapt, we are respectful and unwilling to break away from the customs and traditions we encounter. And the neighborhood lives on according to the white, American, heterosexual, protestant dogmas it has set for itself.

Even taking into consideration the hundreds of racial and cultural variations that have been mixed up in this melting pot, these dogmas are now commonly perceived as "American" and adopted as such. By those living here as well as those living abroad, thanks to songs, literature, movies, etc... They have become a model we have all followed and chosen to take up wholeheartedly.

Like Christmas in Italy: don't we all decorate Christmas trees, invent incredibly difficult tasks for Father Christmas, rush around for hectic Christmas shopping? And in the last few years, haven't all cities opened ice skating rinks, built gigantic malls we prowl around in consumeristic dismay, covered facades with decorations and played Christmas hits over and over again?

"Sure, but it's different in Italy. We do the same things, but in a different way," another guest argues.

I have to agree: "Yes, in Italy, we celebrate our rituals more privately."

And, at most, extend them to our family circle, with various regional variations as well as the grumbling and moaning we adopt when we have to conform to any communal task. Whereas Americans come together at these times and joyfully take pride in being part of a community.

"These are all the usual stereotypes," another guest shoots back. "Don't forget, America is also the cradle of protest. Take San Francisco."

The birthplace of all unconventional movements. The place that goes against all waspish righteousness.

For decades now, San Francisco has been rocking the boat of conformity with waves of pure rebellion, and outrageous outside-the-box jibes.

I've been there three times already, in the last twenty-five years, and I've always considered it a small hearth and home kind of place; unlike all the other majestic and energetic big American cities.

The small trams swerve up and down the hills like a sort of urban rollercoaster, cutting through well defined neighborhoods, identified according to their traditions: Italian, Chinese, the port, the hippies...

"The houses are all different, with unmatching colors!"

Also true. Shapes and paint colors all competing for "the most outlandish" prize. The ancient little houses, for example, standing next to one another, with their brightly colored front doors, embellished door frames, decorated drainpipes and variedly moulded railings alongside little front doorsteps.

Or the most exotic parts of the city, such as the Chinese district, where the red and gold stucco decorations, lanterns and dragons, cover all the facades. As if the furnishings we are used to seeing in a kitsch, touristy Chinese restaurant had burst out onto the streets and covered them with mind-boggling paraphernalia.

And especially everything left over from the 70s, such as the rows of shops doing their best to dazzle customers with the most outlandish gadgets: wigs of various colors, second hand clothes from different eras, costumes of all sorts, out of print books, all shapes of chillum, tattoos, vinyl gems...

Everything is competing to win the top price for eccentricity.

Apart from having to give the kids awkward explanations for some of the objects in the shop windows and a few cafés, none of it stirred any great feelings in me.

"These places are just like they were years ago," I realize. "Just more worn-out, with more listless people."

"What about the hippies? Are they still around?"

"No, when I went last summer, there weren't any."

All that remains of the movement which made everyone feel as free as the air and even more optimistic than Dorothy in The Wizard of Oz, are a few flower painted VW vans here and there.

The movement made of powerful songs and strong colors, chemical dreams and universal love, has faded away and cooled off. It didn't build anything, just slapped a bit of color onto some streets and into a few songs. But it still echoes out of deep corners of the souls of those who caught a glimpse of it and were even just partially grazed by its shock wave. Who saw their older brothers take off with a backpack and hitchhike or walk across the US, stopping off in homes where everything was in common and playing songs on guitars which had been bought with every last penny.

Everything was easy, allowed and possible. It must have been some sort of powerful collective trip. Clinging on to a life made of imagination, living a fantasy, like trying to hold onto a happy dream before waking up.

People in San Francisco keep their eyes shut and clench their fists: still immersed in the dream of those living outside-the-box and against the system.

Actually, there is something left of the dream: the need to differentiate themselves from others, not run with the pack and judge according to conscience and nature. Every last one of them.

How could they not, after all?

"Think about it, the high-minded reactionaries are banned from San Francisco just like the freaks from our Bethesda suburbs."

The collective rebellion. All said and done, even the need to astonish and live outside-the-box has become standardized.

Modifying what needs to be modified, even San Francisco lives up to the American dogma. Everyone complies, paying tribute to the prevailing collective rite which, in this case, is extravagance.

Winter

What upsets me most is that the snow, we had so wished for, hasn't fallen. The cold slaps every other day. Clear, cold days—suddenly slipping in between warmer, rainy spells— sting with beautiful sunlight and stiff air. The other days, instead—when the sky decides to harbor then release aqueous vapors from its belly of clouds—it's rather warm, with thin rain sticking to the skin and grey skies crushing our moods.

Winter has just set in. Tree trunks are bare, hedges dry and colors opaque.

The dead plants are secretly stirring, hiding a seemingly halted life which in fact bears one speck of energy at a time through each day and each bout of bad weather. Flowing under the surface and storing it, as well as transforming it, making it ready to blossom in a few months' time.

Seeing dead vegetation and knowing it will soon come back to life is mind-boggling. Little by little, undetected, its strength holds out and throbs, submerged in nature's fibers.

I too work slowly and almost in secret. I hardly even admit to myself that I have started dreaming again and taken on commitments, weaving together my many ventures made of encounters, hopes and ideas. A foolish and stubborn lymph tickles deep down inside me and sets back into motion the forces which persist in leaving no job undone, even though I have no job.

Wishes, expectations and investments with no returns are back. Notwithstanding the frowning denial of reason, my nature—the core of my old stick—has gained the upper hand. It has become sturdy. Overcoming winds and storms, it has toughened up all its misconstrued beliefs. Writing. Publishing. Organizing events. Productive times are already somewhere in the lymph flowing inside me. Not yet present, but there nonetheless. I can feel them taking up room in the future before even being able to plan them.

It's cold today and I notice something different at the bus stop: we aren't cold any longer. We've got used to it and no longer walk out looking like arctic explorers. Even with temperatures slightly above or slightly below zero, we face the shallow morning winds hatless and gloveless. And finally recognize our German neighbors as equals now that they have decided to don themselves with slightly more adequate coats, having maybe been struck by a bout of bad health.

At the usual bus stop again, with the usual trivial early morning comments.

I say goodbye to the kids and the driver, watch the yellow bus grow smaller along the traffic congested avenue. I think about the sticks and the messed up lymph flowing through me.

I go home, walking through small clouds of breath, greeting the dry, patient trees nursing spring in the recesses of their trunks.

I look deep inside myself and see my own marrow, alive and well; I'm not dismayed by the inconsistent and stubborn ideas being produced by my lymph. It flows, benign, at winter's bountiful slow pace.

CHAPTER VI

Pilgrimage

The sky above our heads is vast. Low and grey, tousled with dark clouds, it's somehow trying to set a limit to the immense Mall: the heart of Washington, made up of monuments, rows of trees, lawns, white buildings and slow wayfarers.

The immense, grey sky seems tired of having to embrace the whole of this incredibly long expanse where our gazes get lost and our souls are disheartened.

"Can we really not get there by bus or subway or whatever?" my visiting mother-in-law asks me.

I shake my head and throw a hard stare ahead. The number of miles we still have to walk to get to Capitol Hill mustn't be revealed; they must be crossed, in silent dismay, promising my mother-in-law we can do it.

"There's no little café or bistro we can stop at on the way?" she retorts.

None.

The virtue of this location, wielding and celebrating power, mustn't be blotted by such frivolous comforts.

"But, if you want something to eat, you could join the queue at that little stand selling Coca Cola and fries."

"No, thank you."

Soon after, my mother-in-law declares: "I need a rest," and sits down on a bench.

The grey sky doesn't give a damn about spring being on its way; it has decided to hand us a fair bit of damp iciness, and showers it down on us with a spray of water.

We look at the buildings around us from our resting place. They stand far away from one another, lined up in tidy, wide, white and grey rows. With wide open spaces between one building and another, between an avenue and a bench, a tree and a sidewalk. The museums and seats of government set so artificially apart from one another it looks like a joke, a miscalculation.

Capitol Hill is all the way down there, lost in the distance.

So far away from the White House, half a city could have been built in between them. Instead, these sites for powerful men and inescapable decisions simply look out over this great lawn with tree-lined avenues and the constant toing and froing of worn-out and thirsty pilgrims.

The Lincoln monument, after all our walking, has fled to the end of the prospect and become almost invisible. Whereas when we were standing at its feet, and when we climbed to the top of the very long stairs, the statue was so big we could hardly capture all its majestic integrity. So we would end up lingering on the gigantic foot, the knotty fingers arching over the handrest of the colossal armchair, or the nostril the size of a saucepan.

Now, the large footed giant is so far away we can't even see it: lost beyond the lawn, behind the obelisk. Even the obelisk. When standing beside it, its whiteness towers as high as a missile being launched, whereas, from where we are now, it looks as tall as a straw, and the State banners, hoisted in a circle of flagpoles at its feet, bring to mind cocktail flags stuck on toothpicks.

Today is obviously not a day for dignified observations. The empire's monuments seem to inspire only snarky comments.

"Shall we go on?" my mother-in-law suggests, having regained some color in her cheeks as well as some strength and a smile.

"Sure!" and I smile too, trying to regain some enthusiasm.

But it's not happening. My critical thinking has got the upper hand and is skipping over everything it sees like a churlish imp. As if a gargoyle from a medieval cathedral had come to life and started climbing all over the blocks of stone.

He points out things and sneers: "Really? You like this stuff?" indicating the very very long and very very wide volumes which could have come out of a creepy fairytale or the warped shapes of a dream.

Maybe it's the pasty weather on this cold, dampish day, that's gluing ugly impressions onto everything. Still, I have the feeling that the excessive amplitude is actually quashing the grandeur it's meant to evoke.

Now, turning himself into an architect, the imp is measuring, between thumb and index finger, the spread out buildings, and whispering in my ear: "They would have been more majestic standing next to one another."

Admittedly, I think being looked down upon by the vast, serious, facades of smooth marble would have been more powerful than observing them separately, so far away from one another, in this limitless vista. Buildings which interact directly with an observer, are much more bewildering.

Like in New York, where the skyscrapers bend over your head. They surround you, grab your chin and lift your gaze, up and up, along miles of glass and concrete; rushing up tens of floors at a time until reaching the sky. Making you address the clouds directly and lend an ear to the great endeavors of all those hard-working little ants who came together to build and lift one bucket, one ladder and one shovel at a time, up to where the air becomes thin.

The pictures of the first building sites show workmen on their lunch breaks, their legs hanging over the void, not giving a damn about their primordial fear of heights, even scoffing at their survival instinct.

It can't have only been the money urging them to work hundreds of feet above the ground. It becomes obvious in the recollections of the Roaring Twenties: those guys had smiles in their eyes and a mocking devil in their souls. They couldn't have cared less about death.

I always get a weird feeling when I'm in New York. Every time I go, I feel everything is crushing down on me: the skyscrapers, voices and car horns, the grayness and fumes coming out of the manholes and the smell of hotdogs, the enormous shop windows and billboards with brightly lit ads...

And the townhouses, thin trees, crowds, loonies and bums surround me, brush up against me, overwhelm me and above all pull me in: they grab me and shove me into something that stirs and floats in the air, that thinks, dreams and lives intensely. All it takes is to wander through it all and you're already part of it, amplifying it with something of your own: one more little note in the symphony, another cog in the wheel.

Even when I'm just passing through, a lost tourist, I feel I'm smack in the middle of it all in New York. I always feel I belong. Even if I don't really know what it is I belong to.

Maybe simply to the idea of being there, all together, tuned in and moving on. Developing, investing, painting, dancing, selling…

Yes, this is the strong emotion I get every time I go to New York, the secret it flaunts at every corner of the very long avenues: the miracle of humankind agreeing and developing, inventing, listening to reason and enduring, gently elbowing its way down the sidewalk.

And erecting skyscrapers, billboards and parks as big as a city within the city… The turmoil of the dawn of civilization: living together, bargaining, meeting one another and setting out rules. A turmoil which, in this city, due to the build up of people and surge in dimensions, has gone so far it overwhelms visitors with a peculiar, fascinating kind of dismay.

New York's powerful, pulsing breath stems from this pact, this primordial miracle. It makes one feel the power that differentiates us from amoebas and beetles: the heartfelt feeling of being together, and becoming creative.

I bat my eyes. I'm not in New York. I'm on the Mall and by my side are tidy rows of lifeless museums, Capitol Hill far ahead, the obelisk far behind and beyond it, even further away, the gigantic Lincoln. Below me, the grass branches out into broad radiuses: from under my feet, for miles, in every direction. Next to me, my mother-in-law is riding out the painful pilgrimage to the Union's most sacred places.

We walk on and I start realizing that, to me, in fact, this white splendor is more like a residue, a worn-out symbol of power. Its creativity stalled in ancient Roman and Greek times: capitals, cornices, pediments, and gables. But bigger, longer, larger and more disquieting than any other ancient building.

That's what happens, I say to myself, when, at the end of the 18th century, you hand a French architect such a vast swampy expanse, far from healthy sea breezes; boiling hot in the summer and freezing in the winter, flat and barren. No history, no trade. No one.

Like a gigantic blank sheet where blocks of stone and marble are called upon to represent abstractions: Power. Civilization. Law.

I can see him scratching his head, poor old Pierre Charles L'Enfant, and then looking for inspiration. What's he supposed to do with all that empty space? He bows down to it and pays tribute: acknowledging its indisputable superiority, he restricts himself to embellishing it with a few monuments and halls of glory here and there.

Crouching over his blueprint, he draws excessively long lines. Taking everything wonderful and majestic France has to offer and throwing it onto a large, empty, sickish land.

*Et voil*à, Washington is born!

"I didn't expect it to be so imposing. It's impressive!" my mother-in-law declares. Her nose in the air, with swollen feet, and shoulders stooped by the fatigue, she's livened by the challenge of regaining each and every one of the monuments glorifying the United States.

"We, in Europe, think they are in decline, but they actually seem as powerful as ever!" she adds.

Which just goes to show how wonderfully varied humankind can be, and how my impressions are, possibly, only my own. Not only, they are also drawn in a gloomy filigree: the awareness of the party being over.

The imp curls his lip, lowers his head and scoffs at me: "I knew it! You're not crazy about all this marble, but it's a part of you, it's in your DNA: it's so European… Sure. You've seen it all before, over and over again, it's old, outdated and shabby! There's so much more out there in the world: millions of people who know nothing about the rule of law, secular justice, Judeo-Christian codes, customs and ideologies. No, wait, sometimes they do know them, but don't give a shit about them! You've seen them, haven't you? Millions of them, right?"

I've seen them, by the millions. In Africa and the Middle East. People who don't dress, don't talk, don't listen and don't even think along the lines we consider so commonplace and universal.

"Right, then look at China, or the whole of Southeast Asia: it's a completely different kettle of fish, and there's so much more, and more modern stuff too. But we are still here admiring a tympanum!"

It's dismaying. All the desolation hidden under the marble's glow.

Then again, that's the way the cookie crumbles. Nothing can be done about it. I can't just give up my Eurocentric and Western point of view because I've travelled around here and there or because I've read a few projections of future economic figures.

You can't just pick up the science books, the ones with drawings of primitive men looking almost like monkeys, then becoming a bit less hairy and standing straighter, and then with a smaller jawbone and bigger head, and so on, over various eras, until the peak of evolution: the white man.

You can't just take those science books and change things to show that monkeys, through genetic selection—over thousands of years, extinctions and biological survival tactics—evolved into a new man, more suitable to the future: beardless, yellow-skinned and with almond-shaped eyes!

The critical imp is scoffing, laughing and having the time of his life:

"Why not? Thousands of people in the Far East of the planet snap up America's economic model (*only* the economic model) and nibble at some new technologies from all over the world. They pour it all into the cocktail glass of their past and their culture, and mix it up vigorously; what do you think it's going to become?"

An expansion beyond all possible predictions.

"And what's it going to taste like, in a few years time, huh? Who knows! It may soon get flushed down the gut of some western-style crisis. Everything down the sewer. And, at that point, what will be left of their culture and their past? Then again, they may also get ahead… what then?"

Who knows what will come out of that cocktail glass, what kind of civilization, what sort of human beings.

New languages, new art, new technologies, new morals... How long before we too start watching new kinds of oriental style movies, on our screens over here. Or hear exotic sounding songs being played over the radio. Fashion with different cuts and different colors. Talking with new tones and adopting new perceptions... How long?

Then I get bored of thinking and shoo critical thinking away. I just want to walk, enjoy my mother-in-law and our visit.

The crooked imp prances off but I hear one last snigger lurking in the air:

"Yeah, have fun, visiting the ruins!"

When you're exhausted, there comes a time you go beyond exhaustion and your feet just step in front of one another, moving forward without measuring distances. Similarly, the thoughts of a tired brain just continue twisting from link to link; but they lose their sharpness, their edge gets chipped and they become their own casualties.

So, while all I want is to enjoy our excursion in peace and quiet, my mind is remembering the manly, proud and strong voice welcoming passengers on arrival at the airport when we flew back to the States after our first visit home, in Italy.

It wasn't addressing all passengers, just the Americans coming back from different parts of the world:

"Citizens of the United States, Welcome Home!" it said. But the voice echoed with a tone that gave a much clearer underlying message: "Dear citizens, after having roamed through god only knows what dangers and deficiencies, you can finally relax: you are now back in the coolest and most equal country in the world!"

The message was repeated every five minutes.

The message and the tone were both a bit shocking because they were being blared out above the heads of hundreds of citizens, who had just landed from the four corners of the earth, for the whole two hours it took to get through the security checks.

So many of those passengers weren't even American and

each one of them, blinded by the same love a mother cockroach has for her child[7], had left a country they found so beautiful.

One could have thought that, maybe, those passengers to whom the message was not being addressed, but were feeling it booming in their chest cavity every damn five minutes, maybe they could have been slightly bothered.

Perhaps they had slept badly in the very uncomfortable second class seats of an American airline and waited in the two hundred person queue for the only bathroom available because the other restrooms were only for the other classes: Almost First, First and Super First.

And witnessed the resounding argument between an Italian passenger, a sociologist, and the crew: mostly standoffish and absolutely uncompromising in defending the rights of the thirty-odd passengers in the First classes to pee in their six restrooms.

And then heard the sociologist's comment on the abuse of space by the First classes as an emblem of what is taking place in American society, with the few rich becoming fewer (only 2% of the population) and richer (holding 80% of the national wealth) and, above all, more and more arrogant.

And ended up thinking about her comment for the next eight hours of their trip, while stifling their need to pee.

Therefore if the non American passengers were upset and their hearts still hanging from the wings of the plane because they were already homesick for that cherished cockroach-child-country of theirs, why blast down on them, with such nagging pride, a welcome home message which didn't concern them?

Or was it some brilliant tactic or super sophisticated CIA torture, put in place to test the passengers? If one of them made some out of control arm movement towards one of the two thousand sharp objects one is not allowed to take on board but which, being angered, he would instinctively look for in his backpack or carry-on bag, then he could be identified, kidnapped and immediately taken to a secret base to be interrogated in various non conventional ways.

However nonsensical, this was the only rationale my mind could come up with, there and then.

Now, many months and thoughts, visits to ruins and imps later, the axis of this episode has tilted and I see it under a different light.

My mother-in-law and I have finally reached Capitol Hill, the cupola, wide stairs and white columns which people around the world know so well. It almost tugs my heart to still feel such awe for the Congress of the United States, which has been honoring, for the last two hundred years and more, the world's first modern democracy.

Thinking about everything that is about to invade and dislodge the columns, the marble and everything they represent, the arrogant welcoming airport message no longer feels like an aggressive reiteration of their superiority, rather like playing defense. The need to puff up its chest and raise its voice because, by now, when it comes to morals, money and ideas, the United States can no longer truthfully say it is the one and only and the best.

Everything's OK

Some days you can breathe gratitude, mixed in with the other gases in the air, as if it were pure oxygen, enlivening impressions and bringing about an elated acceptance of everything around you.

It could happen one Sunday morning, for instance. With roads slightly warmer and spring having dipped its fingertips in pots of paint and strewn a few drops here and there on the grey shrubs.

A day we walk out of our comfortable house, well fed and well shod, feeling safe and free, to join some friends at their house.

You can't always take all this for granted. Can't always be so sure. It wasn't always this way and, in the future, who knows?

In Syria, the regime's grip, pollution, water rationing, religious dogmas and social restrictions became tighter and tighter, gripping our heads, like a garrote squeezing out the joy. Despite the fondness of our Arab friends, leaving felt like making an escape.

In Senegal we were worn out by the exotic illnesses but, most of all, by the scenes of misery around us. The past and our guilty white conscience nagged us, as did the gazes of the locals, making us feel out of sorts because our normality had become an insulting luxury. And a state of impotence.

Sooner or later, there will be another country, after the United States, a new host welcoming us into its existence. How much gratitude, how much joy, will we feel?

I walk down the street to our friends' house, with a cake in hand, feeling rested and safe in the neighborhood where, once, catholics and Italians weren't allowed to live but are now welcomed with big smiles. I'm filled with lighthearted happiness and open to love and gratitude. I'm happy to have received the invitation, and of knowing I can get there without facing any danger or inconvenience.

I sit down, smile at our Italian hosts and their many American guests.

I try to adapt to the tolerant, quiet and tactful ways of the latter. Even when the conversation turns to matters which call for some brazen comment, I stop myself and stifle the outbursts of energy I've inherited from my Tuscan ancestors. Those caustic replies we, in Tuscany, wash down with our mothers' breast milk soaked in a fondness for rash wisecracks and one liners.

They would be considered reprehensible in respectable circles. Especially in these neighborhoods so full of educated, affluent and tolerant people; the neighborhoods with the highest density of culture, affluence and tolerance in all of the United States.

We all know there are much richer people out there, but they are exceptions in a sea of affliction. The people in this neighborhood, instead, are mostly upper-middle class. I look around and see quietly resolute faces. Self-sufficient people who work hard, study, are well-informed and respectfully aloof. They eat leisurely while exchanging remarks about the neighborhood, schools, hobbies and the world's economic problems.

They are dressed for the occasion, in casual, well-chosen clothes, with no loud or boorish luxury accessories. They glance at me just enough to place me, understand whether I'm a local or someone still fitting in, whether I could pull any weight in any of the clubs they are already part of. Then decide maybe not, and anyway I'm too pensive and standoffish for them to want to approach me. I can visualize them, always moving around this way: without butting into people's lives. Without any curiosity or reproach for anything that differs from their norm. Always talking softly, casually dressed, exchanging remarks.

I've decided to smile a lot and say little, today, because I haven't got a lot to add to the conversation. I'm not lacking in opinions, but then again, in this context, it would be out of place for me to shoot my mouth off. No one would find it amusing, apart from me.

So I fight back a yawn, glance at my watch and, since there's plenty of time before we go home, I look out over the perfectly mowed, green lawn where the children are playing, without screaming.

Over the next few days, I ponder the soft conversations and the impartial prattling the Americans were using to talk about practically everything. I realize it isn't just a matter of demeanor. People here really do get less angry than us. Their tone of voice reflects their ideas, and the general idea, here, is that everything is going just fine. The system works, so there's no point in bringing it into question; at most, a few things could be tweaked, from time to time.

There are so many things they don't seem to be bothered about which, instead, would drive us crazy.

The links between politics and vested interests, for instance. We know all about it in Italy. That's why it sparks big questions, debates, shows of boisterous outrage in newspapers and on TV, embittered remarks among friends, afterthoughts, heads banging against the wall and the routine anguishing question: "Who's there left to vote for at the next election?!"

And up the pole, from the politician embroiled in private affairs, the craving to clean up the political pool escalates to campaign financing mechanisms and beyond, up to the most distant springs, the very sources of all politics: the Sacred Principles established by the Constitution.

Because we just can't stop at only one specific case, we always need to throw the whole lot into the fire, including our nation's laws.

Sometimes, even going way beyond what actually needs to be done. Because if we just applied the existing rules, the problems could have already been solved. We have excellent principles, and our system could work properly, if everybody just abided by it.

Instead, every time there's talk of cleaning up and renewing, we kick up a gigantic fuss. Meanwhile the guilty party, hidden in a huge cloud of dust, gets away.

But we are definitely not lacking in participation or the ability to put everything into question.

Right now, Romney is making a kill over here. His opponents are less convincing: some are too aloof, others too headstrong, and they're all weaker than him. He repeats his slogan: throwing out Obama, preventing the States from becoming like Europe.

His ideas are absolutely awesome. But his name is also raised and carried through the air by the strong arms of his private wealth, nourished by astronomical amounts of campaign financing—which his opponents could only dream of.

Injected with three times as many ads, interviews, posters and rallies as the other candidates. Aided (in the birthplace of modern democracy!) by the suppression, some thirty years ago, of par condicio: that annoying rule which, in other countries, still imposes equal time and space in the media to all candidates. US candidates can therefore be interviewed and advertised in unregulated ways and for as long as they want. So all contenders get away with campaigning on steroids.

The lobbies spend whole fortunes pulling strings in the seemingly festive race towards the nomination—which is how the election campaign is played out over here. A flurry of trips, parties, conventions, stars and stripes and streamers. A bit pop star tour, a bit village circus; full of colors, marching bands and cheering.

The lobbies are also all up on stage, every time. They openly approach their chosen candidate, roll up his sleeves, inject him with their fortifying nutrients and walk away without saying goodbye. The candidate with the most lobbies gets so many injections he lasts the longest, is the most visible and shouts the loudest into the strongest amplifier.

A collateral effect is that he starts using the lobbies' slogans, talking about the lobbies' needs, forgetting they are often detrimental to several millions of people—but that's just a detail, it doesn't really matter. All those citizens who don't feel included in his speeches might as well just go home.

Another collateral effect of the lobbies' injections is the risk that voters' turnout will be reduced to figures so small we, hypercritical Italians, would have a field day debating.

There's no doubt people are happier knowing corruption doesn't exist in the country they live in; it's every citizen's dream! And since Americans are masters in having dreams and making them come true, they have, very pragmatically, converted the illusion into reality. All it took was a linguistic tweak and the "illegal financing of political parties" became "campaign donation." Magically replacing a nasty, rotten image with a more promising, healthier sounding one.

And once the magic ball starts rolling, it can't be stopped that easily. So, from one to another, that first small change brought about so many other marvelous shifts.

Americans, for instance, with long suffering resignation, put up with all those killed by the never ending series of psychopaths, armed to their teeth, that gush out of the folds of their society to shoot at helpless citizens. And accept, with patriotic pride, that every single year of the past half century or more, their government bears arms against sworn enemies in at least a few countries around the world.

They manage to convince themselves that freedom is a merciless god, exacting his bloody toll, and choose to ignore the sad, radical mavericks who spot foul play in all quarters. Paranoids who call out the interests of entrepreneurs producing weapons, uniforms, victuals, tents, dressings and flags for the army; all unwilling to disarm the psychopaths and live in peace among others.

When all is said and done, they can now thank Divine Providence for sending them a candidate like Romney. Count on him to protect the United States from the oh so dreadful risk of becoming as pensive, suspicious and sagging as Europe. For sure.

Meanwhile spring has sprung

And the world lies there with its mouth wide open, eagerly awaiting. The mild season flies fast over everything, delivering here, dropping there; it puts light and scent, new energies and ideas into every plant, street, animal and person's beak.

At a time when the Earth is nourishing itself, lavishing presents with unwavering love, I feel like being part of it all: I want to touch, watch and smell all the bounty flowing around. I want to put on sweatpants and boots, grab a besom, some seeds and a rake and take on some gardening, as if rejoining a Panic ritual, rushing towards spring's embrace.

My American friend who also wanted to take part in the gardening ritual, is now showing me her hands covered in sores while I try not to look at those on her face.

"Poison ivy. You should always wear gloves and long sleeves for gardening."

There's this nasty plant, over here, which grows in the woods, sneaks into gardens, and when you brush up against it, it burns more sores in you than Jesus had on the cross. Leaving open wounds dripping blood.

"I'm so lucky I found a good job, with good health insurance. I signed just yesterday!"

Otherwise? Blood and tears and open sores?

I'm again amazed by how cool and collected Americans are when faced with their ruthless system.

And I remember the comment made by that Republican Judge of the Supreme Court. One of those remarks lawyers won't forget easily. A historic comment that will be inscribed in legal literature. Which, in the States, is based more on practices and precedents than actual norms: fish out some judge's verdict, given decades ago, cling to it with all your might and you'll win your case, easy as pie.

So someone who just can't stomach Obama's weak attempt at giving everyone a semblance of medical assistance, will certainly pull out the judge's pearl of wisdom again: his comment on the fact no one can force Americans to eat broccoli, right? So they can't be forced to have medical insurance either!

Another American friend sighs, figuring there's no harm in it, as she tells me she'll have to go back to work after only two days convalescing from the life saving operation she's just had. An occluded vein, fainting and the risk of brain damage forced her to submit to an operation as quickly as possible. Now, while the effects of the anesthetic haven't yet fully subsided, she'll have to go back to the office.

"Why?"

I ask as she stumbles around the room.

"My boss refused me any sick leave, I had to take two unpaid days off."

"Only two?"

"I can't afford to take more."

I felt anger flushing my face, thinking about the heartless boss and the US Government letting him get away with it. My friend instead, stunned but untroubled, went to make a pot of tea.

I again thought about how lucky Americans are, hardly ever calling into question their civilization. Always unequivocally proud of what their ancestors have built and what the Judges of the Supreme Court have declared.

Thereby gracefully avoiding to live the way we Italians live: constantly pissed off, from morning to night.

It's also a matter of habit and co-existence. Every country has its blots on the landscape and, walking among them all the time, people don't notice them as much: they see them with the corner of their eye and get along with what they're doing.

In Italy, for instance, we're used to hearing about the mafia, episodes of nepotism, corrupt politicians, entrepreneurs and employees. We listen to all this wonderful news, deep in our own thoughts, allowing the reports to pour like tomato sauce on spaghetti as we watch the one o'clock news.

Here instead the sweet face of the clean, kind boy, hugging his parents, dressed up for his last day of school, playing ball with his friends or pushing his little brother's bike, plants itself like an ice pick in my throat and stops me from even swallowing my own saliva.

Because the kid was killed by someone on a patrol. A neighborhood watch which, in some states, can even be armed, as it was in this case. In many states, white people have it in for black people, and it was one of these places. A nervous move, a prejudice, a pinch on a trigger and there you have it. The sweet boy is in a coffin, and a handful of people around the United States are wondering whether it wouldn't be best to change the laws, in the states where armed watches are allowed. Maybe it's not such a great idea having them go around shooting whoever they want.

But I already know that one of these days, some Supreme Court Judge will raise his wise, white-haired head, and declare: "Can the Government stop me from blowing bubbles with my chewing gum? No, God forbid! So how is it going to stop me from bearing arms and going out on all the neighborhood patrols I want?"

To each country its own science fiction.

Responsibility

Where I come from, just as we all expect to receive medical treatments, any average citizen would find a doctor's total lack of flexibility inconceivable. Whereas here, it seems to be the norm. The American doctor sticks to the rules, schedules and guidelines. He's laid-back because he's legally bulletproof.

So he allows himself to not visit and send home a kid with a broken arm because his office is closing in fifteen minutes and there may not be enough time to finish the visit before shutting the doors. My child, who fell off the slide, has come to this office regularly, spending whole afternoons waiting for check-ups and vaccinations. He's holding his elbow with his hand and can't believe he is being sent home like this, because checking his arm could, possibly, take more than fifteen minutes.

An American doctor can even get away with letting your stitches become ingrown under your skin because you were given them in Italy and, over here, procedures require the doctor who stitches to take the stitches out. When I got back from Italy after my operation, I went to three hospitals, to no avail, and finally managed to get my gynecologist to remove the stitches. She was the least appropriate person, but the only one who gave in to my tearful outburst.

The problem with stitches also goes the other way, as a colleague of my husband realized when he risked bleeding to death because doctors in three different hospitals refused to stitch a wound from an operation performed by a colleague of theirs in another medical centre. That centre had closed, and the poor colleague with a wound which had reopened, left a trail of blood all over Washington before becoming so totally fed up he furiously threatened lawsuits and reprisals. In the end, the fear of retribution, rather than the sense of responsibility, got the upper hand, and they stitched him up.

Responsibility.

A long, serious word. With echoes of something important and drawn out in time. Something demanding, like carrying a heavy weight on your shoulders and making sure you take care of it. A conscientious doctor takes upon himself the taxing onus of an illness and tells the patient: I'll do my best, I'll offer you every existing treatment to free you from it.

But doctors here don't seem to have any moral responsibility: health is not a universal right, and people are mostly interested in not getting caught up in lawsuits.

"It doesn't only apply to doctors," an Italian friend who teaches here tells me. "It's the same with teaching."

"Teaching?"

My friend, a university professor, sighs and explains that professors here have to shy away from taking responsibility for their opinions. They are all expected to be neutral, equitable, unbiased, almost absent. They must make themselves scarce behind methods, records, positive reinforcement and good marks.

"We must protect ourselves from every possible onslaught. Students pay a fortune for every single exam and often have parents who make hefty donations."

So the students need to know exactly what is expected of them, how they'll be evaluated and be assured they can't possibly fail, before facing the horrible ordeal of a test. Professors can be exposed for any abuse in imagination, criticism or judgement they dare to make.

"Once, I vented my frustration to my Dean: 'I teach literature... how can I be neutral? How am I supposed to write a test that doesn't require an interpretation, that could please everyone?' Do you know what he answered? 'It's your problem, I don't want any trouble.'"

Every now and then, American students try their hand at some international test, competing against students from China, Brazil, India or Europe, and their results are mediocre. On those unfortunate occasions, the experts wonder, and the journalists report their heartfelt questions: "Where have we gone wrong?"

Maybe in China, India or Europe, teachers aren't just playing defense. They are trusted and listened to. They take on their students' education, take responsibility for what they say and the opinions they express. Students learn from them, absorb, try to adapt to their expectations, tackle the criticism and correct their mistakes.

"Yeah, in a fairy-tale world. Don't you remember what it was like when we were in school?"

There were the weird tics, the tough personalities, those who flung their neuroses at the students, sure, I remember. They're as stuck in my memory as the scars I got from chicken pox.

Then, growing up, I discovered students weren't the only victims. There are also the people who work in offices, factories, hospitals... Anywhere there's a handful of underlings who become the outlet for some inescapable big cheese to vent his daily discontent on.

But unlike a supervisor or department head, a teacher totes the burden of knowledge and carries it as far as you, you then burden yourself with it and eventually pass it on, in a never ending sequence. It's risky if you misunderstand the mechanism, or when teachers and students don't see eye to eye. If we perceive our teachers as above and against us, the system is thwarted, the transfers get blocked, and, in facing the big, unknown world out there, all we have are a few snippets of our own personal knowledge...

"I just have to remember to never close the door when students come into my office," my professor friend tells me. "A colleague of mine was charged with sexual abuse."

Because he had closed the door.

Part-time eros

Was the student in bad faith? Or did she really feel the closed door made the meeting too intimate or threatening?

As I leave my friend to do some shopping, I think it could easily have been so. Women, here, boldly manifest their trust in their rights. And, as a woman, you don't sense you're carrying around a body posting messages of availability, attraction and enticement, like in Italy. You're nondescript, as you wander around, unless you actually make a big effort to stick those messages to your body.

At which point you go out shopping with your girl friends, as these teenagers in front of me are doing, in a street in Bethesda's tiny centre. After their shopping spree, they'll probably spend a girly afternoon painting their nails and fixing their hair. Then, happy as larks and giggling away, they'll get all dressed up, climb into heels they're not used to and, on unsteady feet, too colorful and brazen to be casual, they'll tote around their evening-out womanhood, full of enticing signs of availability, and make themselves visible. With a cheerful but slightly naïve, goofy and childish erotic charge.

Women who are a bit older than these girls, instead, go to places intended for people to meet, gatherings where anything can happen, where everyone can loosen up, propped up by a few drinks and the safe knowledge they are all there to meet other people. No one will be shocked if they are approached and no one will be taken to court. Places where, on some occasions, you can indulge and fool around. It's easy to hook up with strangers and end the night the way you want. Everything is allowed, within certain precise boundaries.

But walking down the street the next morning or back at work, those same people would never dare play a seduction game. They won't steal a glance or bat their eyes, take a pose or change their tone of voice. Everything has to go back to a neutral normal.

And I believe this is another custom my fellow countrymen wouldn't appreciate. No playing games, no jousting, no little vibes between men and women...

Because, all things considered, that's what it's all about: appearances, attitudes and looks. In Italy, when a man and a woman look at one another, the first things they see are a man and a woman.

They check one another out, gauge and discern one another, and both make their presence felt, within that space and as a consequence of their manhood and womanhood. Here, beyond the bounds of the times and places dedicated to meeting people, the first thing Americans seem to notice is the fact they are a postman and a female client, or a male teacher and a child's mother, a Mr. Smith in unit A and Mrs. Brown in unit B… And, only then, which race, religion or community they belong to.

And eventually the fact one is a man and the other a woman.

Make way for the next generation

Shopping in the house and garden department store, I'm being helped by a boy who could be my son.

He's earnest and committed in handing me my shopping and, as I place it in the trolley, my mind shifts; the young American, the store and its goods flicker for a second and are suddenly replaced by an Italian store: the colors, faces and Italian goods and the Italian version of the young shop assistant who has just helped me. If he were old, he'd be there topping up his pension fund. If instead he were young or middle aged, this would be his real job, possibly handed down to him over generations.

I can't imagine the Italian version of this whiskerless youngster fretting to become part of the active, productive and salaried society.

In Italy, a similar situation would only be seen in certain places, certain jobs, within certain social classes. Here, instead, it's part of the landscape, as are lawns, porches and smiles.

Youngsters here have a strong work ethic. It's standard for them to make a bit of cash doing little jobs, even as kids still living with their parents. And later support themselves through college doing small, badly paid jobs with no guarantees. And if they are not studying, they're truly open to all opportunities. By our standards, they are often exploited unfairly, which would outrage us Italians but, again, it doesn't seem to bother Americans.

It's not only about paid work: kids often sign up as voluntary assistants to help their schoolmates at pedestrian crossings on the first days of school; voluntarily organize end of the year school parties, volunteer to collect funds for charities or clean up plastic and other waste along river banks.

It's called Community Service and it's instituted to reinforce the idea everyone can contribute to making the whole system run smoothly. They even get extra credits in their school reports for it, so they all do it.

Where I come from, people seem to think civic mindedness emanates from some inborn, altruistic, generous and compassionate part of one's soul. It's great if you have it, but if you don't, too bad for you. And while we expect our kids to grow up by themselves—or possibly with some miraculous intervention—into conscientious, responsible citizens, we complain about their laziness, indolence and lack of awareness of real world problems. But we don't consider sending them out to shovel snow, hand customers their shopping or help classmates on their first days in school.

We Italians don't like menial jobs. They're a sign of wretchedness, a stain on the family's history. We like to think our kids will never have to start at the bottom of the ladder.

Yet, by now, they are bound to be trainees for the rest of their lives. And when they finally make it onto the real job market, weaving through trial and error, promises and changing laws, they'll have turned thirty in the batting of an eye and still be working as shop assistants.

But I suspect it's not just a matter of social pride. We are the ones averting their eyes from the adult world, putting it off, to the point of almost deleting it, because we ourselves don't like it, sometimes even hate it. So how could we possibly want to impose it upon them?

And it's not just about work, it's also about our concerns for the community, understanding the consequences of our actions, humility and the pride in completing a task… All this seems so taxing to us, heavy-going and suffocating. Things that curb our talent and our free spirit. Which only jerks would do.

Here instead, young kids are conscientious and hard-working. They wouldn't tear a blade of grass in a public park and they respect private property more than the Bible.

The United States is a tough teacher. Babes still in swaddling clothes are hit over the head with the importance of accomplishment and the need to step up their game. They aren't allowed to waste time, complain or walk away from a stumbling block. They mustn't cheat. They are given a tidbit of guidance then sent off into the art room to deal with the clay of life: "It's hard, guys, but it's all yours. Get started!"

"Can I lend you a hand outside, Ma'am?" the beardless shop assistant asks.

I refuse politely. I'm not that old!

I say goodbye to the obliging teenager, pay and reach my car in the typical, comfortably large American parking lot. Then, faced with the gigantic amount of things I've just bought, I regret declining his help. I sigh and start transferring everything into the boot of the car.

A group of kids with school bags on their shoulders walk past me on the sidewalk. And thereafter, a mum hurries by with three little boys, each carrying his own sports bag.

Even when they're not working, kids here are like that: always busy, going somewhere or on their way home from something. By subway or by car, quickly hurrying along. Forging through hours of sports or homework, grinding tests and community service, taking part, competing, contributing…

Sometimes these kids and their super-efficient parents are just too much.

Especially for the Italian adolescents relocated here, who miss the lazy hanging out, getting together for no real reason and chatting, playing with glances and incitements, laughs and nonsense.

Wasting time as in a sport, or a very refined form of art which allows a void to be filled with everything that can produce a thrill rather than just be useful.

In fact, I can't stop thinking that maybe in between a commitment, a match or homework, a bit more healthy *dolce far niente* wouldn't be a bad idea, over here. It could inspire creativity, the simple getting together and priceless eking out of words and sensations, while seeking some arcane form of amusement.

"They are too restrained and disciplined when they are kids and when they get a bit older, on some occasions, they just lose control, actually they tear themselves out of control. They get completely drunk, behave like thugs, have sex without even knowing what they're doing."

This is what an ex high school teacher had to say, one day, about American high school kids.

And what happens on university campuses literally gives me the shivers. Where the various fraternities have developed sadistic and violent initiation rites, with adverse codes of behavior in which drug or alcohol induced highs, coercion, humiliation and loss of control rule a life that runs parallel to classes and exam results. And excellence has nothing to do with shining.

Slackening the grip could really help. If having fun were less disciplined by schedules and precepts, kids could actually relax more and just enjoy themselves without feeling the need to dull their senses or become aggressive. Without having to wait until campus life to live a sort of "no man's time" in which all that was forbidden before, suddenly becomes possible, right up to graduation. To then fall back into a life made of commitments, responsibility and scheduled amusement.

Couldn't they enjoy some mild infractions and a bit more freedom with their feelings and behavior a little bit sooner, in a milder form, a bit more forever?

But that's not the way it goes. Kicking afternoons around is for outsiders, city boys who've grown up in the shadow of housing projects, who are never accompanied and least of all taught. Underprivileged kids who do only that: mess around. Or, at other times, destroy themselves, the streets they live in and other people's property. They've been cut out of the system, they don't fit the successful bill, because they don't even know what it is; they've never even heard of the rules that help people grow up and thrive in the American way of life. They just get by, in the city, demeaning themselves and everything around them, amid dangers and fights for survival that are more exacting than building a future.

Strangely, the street corners they live on look a lot like the street corners of so many of our Italian cities, which are neither poor nor degraded, but where kids are nonetheless driven to dirty and destroy, disrupt and disturb. Just like babies who haven't actually grown up, with no one ever demanding or expecting anything from them. Kept away from the ugly, nasty and stifling world of adults, they grind through their days spray painting, invading pavements, yelling and gurgling disjointed sounds.

My trolley is empty and the car boot is full.

I catch the door handle and as I pull the car door shut I think about the world that's being built in Italy, in those streets being degraded by regular kids. I have a sudden dizziness. What is it that's unfolding slowly, day after day, spray can after spray can, shout after insult? I fear it'll be a future of glee without happiness. A future of challenges without dreams.

So many suicides in Italy

One, two, even three people a day. The world economic crisis has reached them too. It has torn their jobs from their hands and shred them to pieces. So they couldn't pay their debts, installments, or buy food for their families. Finally, after having lived hanging over the precipice of hardship for a bit, they let go and flew out of life.

We are so weak in the face of hardship compared to Americans...

Here, hurricanes and earthquakes, financial catastrophes or a boss's whim, pressure everyone to always have their shoulders pinned to the ground and their heads over the abyss.

"I'm sorry I didn't warn you sooner but we are moving."

My Italian student neighbor told me a few days ago with a rushed smile.

"That's why I haven't been coming to our lessons lately, I was too busy."

"It's not a problem, please, don't worry about it. I'm just sorry you're leaving."

"Me too, but we need a bigger place…"

Which sounded a bit strange for a couple who live alone in a house with two floors. On the other hand—I reminded myself—Americans are obsessed with their houses, so maybe this couple was just a bit more so.

Then, the neighbor with the dachshunds told me the true story. He came hastily over to me as I was pruning the plants, and whispered: "It's not true they wanted to move. Their house went into foreclosure!"

I was flabbergasted. Shocked by the way the wheels of fortune truly turn in a whiff, over here. By how someone can turn sixty and end up with nothing. And how strong and unruffled my sixty-year-old neighbors looked despite having lost everything.

There's this sort of bravery, around here, of determination in the face of adversity, that we Italians can only dream of. I get the shivers simply watching others go through disasters. And become dismayed in seeing the church torn down by the earthquake, or the town hall in Emilia crumbling like a cookie. My thoughts rush to the Government, which has no money left. What's going to happen? How are the people who lost their jobs in the destruction going to support themselves? I get completely overwhelmed. And envy those on this side of the ocean who are hardly ever overwhelmed by anything.

Instead of giving up hope, Americans get insured. Against catastrophes, illnesses and break-ins. Those who can, protect themselves with insurances. And those who can't, lose everything, and that's that. They know the rules which are, as always, clearly spelt out. So, faced with the pile of wooden beams and torn fabric that make up the remains of his home, or the heap of dreams and disappointments that were the essence of his job, faced with everything he can lose, the American has the innate strength of his solitude, as always. So he rolls up his sleeves and starts over again. Without complaining about his loss.

Always pioneers. In the face of crises, or catastrophes. Without taking it out on others or God, they concede and march on, looking for new places, new resources. And that's what saves them: pursuit and hope.

Whereas for us, being torn from our usual lives is so painfully devoid of possibilities and solutions it leads us to death. Because our lives are niches we've built with our hands and the patient hands of our ancestors, a small space we have scrambled for and passed on, defended and fenced in. Losing it is an overwhelming sorrow.

Here, instead, they don't have niches, the landscape is open. You find and lose, conquer then leave behind.

Setting aside the great lineages and the phenomenal ruling families, of course. Those guys have lots of niches. Actually, they're more like caves and mountains full of tunnels. Which they've conquered and held on to tightly, inch by inch, through wars, hard work, craftiness and lucky strokes. In hard times, their heirs are the guys who jump off the family skyscraper.

But the average Americans, who haven't got the burden of accumulated and bequeathed wealth, who make up the majority of the country, all have some kind of talent, gift or training, even just basic training, that could be useful to someone else. They'll find a job; a corner to survive on and start over, after each crisis or catastrophe.

Because there's a constant transfer going on here, an exchange of goods and abilities. With no barriers, unrelated to fraternities, family and political ties or bonds of friendship. It's this endless opportunity which allows them to live and prosper, within their harsh and ruthless economic system.

The very system we are blindly importing, little by little. But without a speck of their transparency and work ethic. We're allowing the average deviousness of everyday citizens and the great roguishness of powerful Italians to be unleashed onto the free market.

May the guardian forces of the Universe be with us.

There seems to be no envy here. People rejoice over what someone achieves, showing absolute involvement in their success — at least on the outside: if they do become green, they never show it.

How much do you make a year? It would be an indecent, annoying and almost disrespectful question where I come from. If you're rich, you feel ashamed, or fear the IRS; if you're poor, you feel ashamed or fear someone is going to ask you for a loan, because there's always someone worse off than you. There's none of that here. Here there's a much wider sharing of knowledge and information: your grandma's recipe, where you bought that dress, an opening for a research position, a translation job, a book publishing, how much I spent on my car, how much I make per year...

Because if I have the power to grant you something, and you are up to the task, then there you have it, the deal is on. Nothing shady or reprehensible.

Whereas in Italy, it's all a matter of factions. If I have the power, I won't let go, won't share it with anyone, or, at best, I'll broaden it to a tiny circle of guys like me: blood relations or interested parties.

Here, instead, even those whimsical events that appeal to people interested in literature, spark interest and involvement: "What are you up to? Can I see what you've done? I really like it, hey, guys, come over here: take a look at this!"

In Italy, people are much stingier in showing their esteem and simple sharing is agonizingly difficult.

My fellow citizens over here seem to have adopted the general mood and have become more open, curious and proactive with regards to the skills of others. They go about with their eyes open and arms outstretched, ready to catch what is being thrown at them.

Maybe they didn't actually have to adapt. Maybe they came here because they already knew the atmosphere would suit them better. This was exactly what they were looking for: a place where everyday life is bathed in loyalty. Where people spur one another on, and are always on the lookout for the good side of things, the can-do spirit and audacious endeavors.

Neverland

Summer is wrapping us in damp heat again. It's covering plants in a lush green spread, making animals hurry around and skies open to the light and wind.

"Sunny days that I thought would never end," as the songwriter from North Carolina used to sing.

Days which take me beyond wonder, disappointment and discovery. Carry me into normality and make me feel I belong here, in these streets, these lights and these customs. Through these steady dribbling days, a simple, clearcut question comes gushing out: "Could I, one day, wish to live here?"

Forever. On a permanent basis. Without observing and testing any longer, rather taking action, building and putting everything at stake.

In the past, when I listened to American music, read books and watched movies, I used to imagine doing so. I considered the US a safe port of departure, a land of hope: a place where castles in the air never crumbled because they could always be stoked with new dreams, new awareness.

I used to believe it was a land of endless civil liberties, bringing together unlimited possibilities of change, good judgment and willpower. A place with a great deal of self-consciousness, which perceived the world's problems and sang them, wrote about them and brought them to the screen.

Now I've discovered that hidden behind those songs, words and images, is a harsh land, where several do make it, but only because just a few actually turn around to help the multitude of those who don't.

I realize I probably wouldn't be able to live with that harshness in me. I miss the poor old bankrupt Europe which has been trying for centuries—and sometimes managed—to make things better. That tries to heal everyone and get them all through school, give citizens inspiring surroundings and allow everyone to benefit from nature and art.

No, I probably couldn't live here forever.

But economies in Europe are collapsing. The politicians, nowadays solely concerned with budgets, are flailing through the stormy waters of international balancing acts. They swim with their necks stretched, barely managing to keep above the surface the noses of those nations which are grabbing at their necks. The faces of these European politicians are strained by effort and worries, because these ancient, generous creatures they are trying to save, weigh too much and could actually drown.

Their model doesn't work any more. Preserving landscapes, treasuring monuments, assisting everyone, guaranteeing an education... The chimera is over, the chips are down: both here and there, the only things that count are commercial interests and the free market. Welcome to reality, welcome to the future.

So this is our fate. *Homo homini lupus*: a man is a wolf to another man. But Americans, who some see as outmoded — and I myself have seen lost at a distance, at the tail end of a path humanity has already trudged down — are still role models, still trailblazing. They were the first to adapt to the ruthless laws of nature, of the fittest, most intelligent, shrewdest and most flexible. And he who can't cope gets the short end of the stick, won't manage to impose his model or his needs, and will probably give up the ghost: all in all, a providential way of throwing off dead weight.

I'm probably part of the last generation of those who've been held in the strong arms of a mother welfare State. Which sees and provides, feeds and guarantees. Heals grazed knees, sends you to school and even gives you a snack. But, above all, loves you just the way you are, accepts you and obliges your older and stronger siblings to play with you and help you with your homework.

Mum is dying and we, her kids, will soon be alone in this world.

Each licking his wounds and honing his brain on the arithmetic of his possibilities.

Who knows if the weak one is going to make it, he looks sickly. Some say he'll be fine, he'll learn to sort himself out. The new situation, based more and more on the American model, will do us all good.

I feel regret sticking to the back of my throat. For the way we were. For the way they were in my dreams.

Then again, not even that.

It occurs on a holiday, during a ride along a bike path.

Halfway across a bridge, my fingers gripping the safety net, I watch the cars driving along in their typical flow.

Perched on the bike saddle, not wanting to get off, I wait for the others to catch up and, in the meantime, look down at the crossroads below. My eyes find the exact spot where, a few days ago, a cyclist was lying on the ground surrounded by the usual ten emergency trucks.

That day, we had glanced at the world grinding to a halt.

We'd looked at the exact spot where a man had been thrown to the ground by unexpected events and other men were assisting to avoid him losing everything because of that.

The world had stopped.

Now, cars are driving by and there are other bikers at the traffic lights, waiting their turn to cross the road, without even taking into consideration the idea that, in a few seconds' time, their world could stop.

The light turns red, the flow changes tack, and pedestrians and bikers cross together.

"Mum, here we are!"

"Why did you stop? Are you tired?"

"No, I was just waiting for you…"

"Ok, now catch me if you can!"

I've never resisted a challenge.

I break away from the net and throw my weight into the pedals. Grinding the bike path tarmac, gliding through the park. Under the leaves, passing disciplined joggers.

I push and fend the air, the wind ruffling my thoughts.

And as I watch my kids pedaling fast ahead of me, I think about time, which hasn't stopped. Instead, it always ticks on, trickling out change, after change, after change, like syrup from the bark of a maple tree. I realize something sweet may still come of it all.

The future is born every day. Every moment. We are still in time to take it into our arms, love it and raise it the way we want.

I slow down, pull over and signal to my husband that I'll catch up with them soon.

Now I just want to gaze at the sky, watch the birds chasing the light. Allow a budding idea to stretch out from the centre of my mind; it wants to bloom.

I see the others accelerating, laughing in the distance. In the woods full of strength and the people walking through, worshiping them.

I realize the America I dreamt of and had inside me, has never existed, it has never disappeared. It's the windy corner of my heart where imaginary visions whirl and the persistent craving for something else dwells together with displaced realities and a reinless blues.

How naive of me to think I could find that corner of my heart in a country. How selfish of me, too. Expecting everything from a place, without giving back.

It will all be different from now on, I can sense it. Because I've finally understood what America is all about.

It's the precious tower full of gems floating above reality, made of potential. A dream urging us to find a better way ahead.

America is all in my mind, powerful and endless, present and future, wonderful.

"Hey, wait for me!" my voice smiles out. And without waiting for an answer, I take off at top speed.

Notes

1. In Italy, spring cleanings were followed by the local priest coming to people's houses to bless them before Easter.
2. Latin for "Your death is my life."
3. "... per questi quattro soldi, questa gloria da stronzi," *L'avvelenata* (Poisoned), by Francesco Guccini.
4. "Ferirsi non è possibile, morire meno che mai…" *L'uomo che cammina sui pezzi di vetro* (The man walking on shards of glass), by Francesco De Gregori.
5. "... ognuno col suo viaggio, ognuno diverso." *Voglio una vita spericolata* (I want a reckless life), by Vasco Rossi.
6. "For the city (Rome) and for the world." A standard opening in ancient Roman proclamations.
7. Italian proverb: *Ogni scarrafone è bello a mamma sua* (Every cockroach is beautiful to its mother's eye.)

www.ingramcontent.com/pod-product-compliance
Lightning Source LLC
Chambersburg PA
CBHW071423160426
43195CB00013B/1779